ABANDONED AT BIRTH

Searching for the Arms
That Once Held Me

JANET SHERLUND

Published by Worth Books, an imprint of Forefront Books, Nashville, Tennessee. Distributed by Simon & Schuster.

Library of Congress Control Number: 2024901341

Print ISBN: 978-1-63763-275-8
E-book ISBN: 978-1-63763-276-5

Cover Design by Mimi Bark
Interior Design by PerfecType, Nashville, TN

Printed in the United States of America

*To Rick, Will, Ben, and Caroline, for your love,
compassion, and encouragement.*

CONTENTS

PROLOGUE

Filed Away
2021

I drove to the adoption agency on an unusually warm November day—sixty-five degrees, with bright sun and pure blue skies. Most trees still held their leaves—the consequence of a warm, wet autumn—and the roadside glowed green and gold with only the occasional streak of orange. The radio blasted Springsteen, and I drummed the steering wheel, my mind wandering with the ease of familiar roads. The route took me through the town where my husband, Rick, and I had lived for thirty years and along roads I remembered from my childhood. Given my destination, the drive through my past was poetic. Snugged into my seat, sunlight curling around my shoulders, I was grateful for the opportunity that lay ahead—to read excerpts of my adoption file from 1954.

Eleven years earlier, I took the same drive to the agency while searching for my birth parents. Such information hadn't been offered to me then, but now, many years into a difficult journey, the compassionate social worker thought it might be helpful. While I had since discovered many facts about my adoption, I was looking for nuanced details. Did my mother ever hold me? Have I ever seen her face? Where was I between my birth and adoption? I hoped reading specifics would bring an aha moment of understanding and prayed for much-needed closure. Fortified by all I had learned over the past decade, I walked into the agency with a big smile, confident the pages I read today would be the Holy Grail, the final piece of the puzzle.

Gloria, the social worker, greeted me. We chatted as she guided me into a small, friendly conference room with stuffed animals nodding down from a bookshelf and easy chairs arranged for conversation. She sat across from me, holding some papers on her lap. "I saw the letter this agency sent you in 1977 when you wrote to request information." I nodded, recalling the letter I had written forty-four years earlier, just after college graduation. It asked about my ethnicity, what my birth parents looked like, why I was given up for adoption—*anything* they were allowed to tell me. The agency's reply was breezy and carefully edited. They had privacy agreements to uphold, adoption laws to follow. "I thought it was awful that they didn't tell you every nonidentifying fact from your file. This is your story, your life, and you're entitled to know more." She reached across and handed me what was a summary of interviews with my birth mother. "Take your time reading these. I'll be in my office next door." She slipped out and left me with the faded and discolored documents, some handwritten and some typed pages from 1954. The story of my beginning.

The old paper was covered with the soft dents of typewriter keys and a social worker's neat, professional script. Some pages were stiff and crinkled, others limp. They all smelled musty. When I touched them, it was as if they could transport me back to the day I was born, to the story others knew but I did not.

On the first yellowed page, Shirlie Anne Jones was listed as my "Unmarried Mother." I was listed as her child, Linda Lee Jones, born on July 1, 1954.

My stomach whirled to see that name typed out on the official paper. I was once someone else with another name, another identity.

Eleven single-spaced pages described their interviews with Shirlie and noted how distant she was, how removed from the process. My birth mother first called the agency on July 7, six days after my birth, during which time I remained in the hospital nursery, fed by rotating shift nurses. My mother never saw, fed, or cared for me in the hospital, a fact the agency noted as unusual. They offered her multiple opportunities to see me—a standard practice—but she declined each time, instead asking how soon she could sign the papers for my release. When the baffled social worker finally asked if I was even real to her, she replied, "Frankly, no."

Throughout the paperwork, I'm referred to as "Shirlie Anne Jones's daughter, Linda Lee," and it catches me off guard each time. Being Shirlie Anne Jones's *daughter* is entirely foreign to me, and the idea of my ever having been Linda Lee Jones is bizarre.

On page eight of the notes, there's a paragraph about baby Linda Lee. *Linda Lee has become a very beautiful, alert, and attentive baby. She has blonde hair, blue eyes, and a fair complexion, and is filled out very nicely. She is an alert, happy, emotionally sensitive baby whose present rate of development is definitely accelerated.* I didn't know how to process this description of myself. My life began when I was adopted. I had no concept of my existence at this age or of using that name. And while I didn't identify with her, Linda Lee sounded like a lovely little baby, and I was eager to learn more.

Toward the back of the file, a "Developmental Examination" page caught my eye. At that point, I was in a foster home run by Mrs. Person in Far Hills, New Jersey. A psychologist gave me a Gesell Developmental Scale test to assess my early abilities against normative data. At first, I read it with only passing interest because how much can you tell about a five-week-old infant? But as I skimmed the report, something shifted. It described a very *real* baby, one I saw clearly in my mind's eye. Someone I recognized as myself.

Linda Lee is an alert, happy, emotionally sensitive baby . . . Adaptive, language and social behavior are advanced. Linda attends quickly to the dangling ring when it is held over her chest and follows it well past the midline. She has a relaxed grip on the rattle and gives a specific facial response to sound. Linda is a very social baby. She smiles readily in a play period and gets quite excited when the examiner talks to her. Linda is a well-developed, alert, responsive baby who makes an excellent impression on the examiner.

I could see myself watching the ring and holding the rattle, and the description of me smiling easily, being visually alert, and having a particular facial response was familiar. So were the comments about my being emotionally sensitive, enjoying interacting with the examiner, and making a good impression. I connected with this. I saw myself in that baby and recognized Linda Lee Jones as me.

I was born with traits I still have, and they came from Shirlie Anne Jones and my birth father. I am *their* blood. I came into this world as someone else before I was given a new identity by the people who adopted me and changed my name to Janet Lucile Leef.

A few sentences later, when I read, *Linda Lee Jones was released by her mother on July 30, 1954*, I became unglued. I was officially Linda Lee Jones when I was released, not a vague "Baby Girl Jones" waiting for an identity. I had a name and a heritage. I was Linda Lee Jones, relinquished by my mother—my legal and officially recognized mother, Shirlie Anne Jones, who signed the release form. The social worker noted, "[Shirlie] again did not display any emotion, thanked me for all my help, and said she felt quite relieved."

I couldn't shake the image of little Linda Lee lying in the middle of a crib watching the ring and shaking the rattle for the examiner. She was a newborn alone in the world, sleeping temporarily in a foster home far away from where she started or would end up, waiting for an agency to nullify her heritage and assign her to strangers. My breath caught. I felt small and scared. I wanted to weep for that little lost baby, Linda Lee. For *me*.

Suddenly, the room felt close. I pushed damp hair off my forehead and struggled for air. Shuffling the papers together, I stood, unsure my legs would hold me, and found Gloria in her office. "Thank you so much for letting me read this, Gloria. It really meant a lot to me."

"I know it did." She smiled with an understanding I didn't yet have.

All I wanted now was to get home. I hurried out to the fading afternoon and sat in my car as I gathered my wits to drive into rush hour traffic. There was no looking at foliage color on the drive home or grooving to The Boss. I was melting into unfathomed sadness, sinking into my seat as grief gathered in my brain and dropped through my center like lead. It was excruciating and I didn't know what to do with the intense emotion. It was primal. There was no language for what I felt. There had never been. It happened long ago before I could think in words. I called Rick but could barely speak. "I hurt so deeply" was the best I could do. He stayed on the phone with me for the rest of the drive home. We didn't talk much, but it felt good to know he was there, listening and wishing he could ease my pain, waiting for my car to pull into the driveway so he could wrap his arms around me.

By the next morning every part of me ached, it was difficult to breathe, and my brain was completely fogged. The hurt reverberated through me like the tolling of a large, low bell. In my mind's eye I saw myself lying in the crib, and I repeated the name over and over: Linda Lee Jones, Linda Lee Jones. Who was *she*? Who am *I*? Why didn't my birth mother want me? All connections to my bloodline, my biological family, had been denied. The identity I now held had been randomly assigned through an agency.

Lingering, wordless grief suspended in me like smoke. Pulling on an oversize sweater, I wrapped my hand around a cup of tea and looked out at the sky, my thoughts diffusing into the pale light.

CHAPTER ONE

Unrelated Thoughts

Who am I? What am I? These questions are the strongest memory I had of my childhood. I was a mystery, a person unknown, and it frightened me. I couldn't see my reflection without wondering who I looked like and where I came from. I yearned to hear someone say, "Oh, you look just like your grandmother" or, "You have so-and-so's nose." Anything for a connection to someone real, for an explanation of my existence—how I came to be.

My recollections of childhood are ones of feeling disconnected and confused. I was simply there, in the redbrick house on a quiet street, in a family where no one shared blood. All my siblings were adopted too. We sat at the dining table between the mahogany sideboard and matching breakfront, a family more carelessly assembled than the dinner menu. My brother, Eric, eighteen months older than me, was restless and impatient. Mark, eighteen months younger, was quiet and nervous. Susie, seven years younger, watched us all with suspicious eyes.

Even as a child, I understood the adoption process. It was part of our bedtime story. Once the agency decided where an infant would be placed, the adoptive parents received a call to "come and get the baby." The agency my parents used presented the adoptee to their new parents in an antique cradle with a tall bonnet top. It sat behind ornate pocket doors, which opened with a flourish.

I sensed the serendipity of my life. It was so capricious; nothing about me was solid or sure. Had my name been farther up or down the list, I'd have different parents and siblings and a different name. I might be in a worse family or a better one. I imagined the Cooks' dinner table next door. The Cooks with their dark curly hair, round freckled faces, drinking and dancing. What would it be like to sit among them at mealtimes? Or how about the Stewarts' dinner table in their elegant house with a sign in the driveway that pointed to something called the "Service Entrance"?

But I was here, among this family. Who were they? Who was I?

No one looked or moved like anyone else. We didn't share likes or dislikes, strengths or weaknesses. We participated *with* each other but didn't belong *to* each other. There was a disconnect around the table and you could feel it in the air. Separate force fields surrounded each of us. We were all built from different DNA. Molecules were not shared, and each of us sat in our own genetic dust. It was primal and palpable.

Dad ate quickly and quietly. Mom ran back and forth to the kitchen. Eric kicked his legs under the table and itched to be excused; Mark spilled his milk; and Susie fed herself pickled beets. I wondered where all these people came from as my eyes roamed around the table. Where did *I* come from? I was from stardust or sparks, from a vapor or a thunderclap. I was quicksilver. It was as if I'd been floating on the wind, to light on this family. I had borrowed their identity and name, been taught their interests, and felt the falsehood of that every day.

When I was five, I imagined I was a kidnapped Chinese princess. Looking at my round face in the mirror, with eyes that smiled into slits and short bobbed hair with bangs, I thought I looked just like the

Asian girls in my picture book of *Children around the World*. Those illustrations mirrored me more than anyone I knew in real life, and the Chinese princess identity was as plausible as any other. Maybe I'd been kidnapped and brought to America! Right now, I was sure someone was looking for me and wondered what would happen when they found me. I wasn't afraid of being taken back to China. I believed it would feel like home, somewhere I'd be solid, complete, and safe because when I was reunited with my real family, I'd make sense.

I would stare at myself in the mirror as the questions repeated, "Who am I? What am I?" The endless, unanswered taunts hovered overhead and crashed down on me, looping through my brain until I had a visceral reaction: a jolt of fear, aloneness, and total detachment. I would no longer recognize my reflection and was shocked and scared by how untethered I felt from everything around me. My stomach jumped, a chill spread through me, my heart raced. I felt profoundly alone. I was aware of everyone else in the house and could hear where they were and what they were doing. But I felt like I was a million miles away and they didn't know I was missing.

CHAPTER TWO

The Accommodating Child
1947–1964

How did this random, mismatched family come to be?

My parents, Audrey and Bob, tried to have children for five years before adopting. They met while earning master's degrees from the Stevens Institute of Technology. Mom was the first woman to earn a master of mathematics at that university. Driven and competitive, she was proud to challenge the limitations imposed on women of her time. She grew up succeeding at everything she did and basked in the admiration it brought her.

Mom had a bright smile, was trim and attractive, and walked with a quick, confident step, her skirts swinging flirtatiously around her knees. One day, she caught Dad's attention as she stepped off their commuter train and strode across the platform. "I'm going to marry that gal," Dad announced to his best friend, Hank.

And he did.

The youngest daughter of a working-class New Jersey family, Mom was born unexpectedly at home on July 15, 1922. The night

Grandma Vincentz gave birth to my mom she had no idea she was pregnant, having been told ten years earlier that she couldn't have any more children. Heavyset all her life, she thought her recently expanding belly was just continued weight gain. She was at a friend's dinner party that July evening, seated at the table, when her water broke over the dark Persian carpet. Later that night, Mom made her surprise entrance into the world. With two brothers, fourteen and twelve years her senior, and a ten-year-old sister, Mom was a latecomer to the family, and sadly, the joy of her arrival was soon overshadowed by tragedy.

Before Mom's first birthday, her sister, Sissy, died from scarlet fever and diphtheria. Sissy's death plunged my grandparents into a deep, almost fatal depression. My grandfather walked into the ocean to drown himself until Grandma charged into the waves and pulled him out. When he took to drinking, Grandma soothed herself with food, while the teenage boys found refuge in activities outside the home. Mom grew up in the hollow Sissy left behind and desperately sought the attention of her grieving parents by exceeding in every way. She graduated as valedictorian of her high school at sixteen. Then after four years of college, she began a teaching career, started graduate school, and purchased her own home in Millburn, New Jersey, a highly unusual step for a young woman in the 1940s. The house was a small cottage, green with black shutters, a block from the town park and just down the hill from Millburn High School where she taught.

My father, Bob, was tall and handsome, with a great head of hair and a shy smile. He was the oldest of five in a prosperous Minnesota family. Quiet, kind, and generous, he had a dry sense of humor and tossed out killer one-liners. Grandma Leef once told me he was the only one of her children who never gave her a moment of trouble, not even once. After receiving a bachelor of science degree, Dad traveled east to be an electrical engineer for International Telephone & Telegraph. He loved his work, pursued graduate studies at night, and enjoyed forging a new life in New Jersey.

Mom and Dad married on June 21, 1947, less than a year after meeting. He was twenty-six; she was almost twenty-five. After the ceremony, everyone gathered in Mom's backyard.

Black-and-white home movies show Mom and Dad beaming, surrounded by everyone from their families. Grandpa Leef, Dad's father, stood tall and elegant in his morning suit, his movements reserved and purposeful. Grandma Leef wore a smartly tailored dress and a hat festooned with netting. Grandma Vincentz's suit looked tight; the belted top and contrast stitching emphasized every bulge. She clutched a limp handkerchief in her hand and raised it against her chest as her eyes darted through the crowd. Every now and then she forced a timid smile. Grandpa Vincentz, stocky and compact, walked behind her with a bulldog gait and perpetual scowl. Friends milled about as Dad stepped onto the porch with a handful of oranges and, smiling modestly at the camera, began to juggle. A clothesline strung off the corner of the house appeared in almost every scene, and guests ducked under it or sat beneath it eating wedding cake. At one point, as Dad watched the photographer take formal photos of his bride, he reached up and held the line, bouncing it as absentmindedly as a teenager. Rhododendrons and roses bloomed in front of tall hedges, but nothing trumped the bride's bouquet with its dramatic spray of gladiolas. Mom wore an organza hat with a sweetheart brim and long veil, and despite the summer day, her gown had a heavy lace bodice and long sleeves. A single strand of pearls was fastened around her neck. Dad looked so proud of her as he swept her into his arms, dipped her back, and kissed her passionately.

Mom had a disciplined, athletic body, one she felt in control of, so naturally she couldn't understand why she didn't get pregnant as quickly as her married friends. She was devastated by her failure to conceive.

As the childless years mounted despite the help of specialists, Mom looked for alternatives. She knew a lovely couple, a doctor and his wife, who had adopted a little girl, and she broached the subject with Dad one evening at dinner.

"Bob, I think we should adopt a child. The Savages adopted little Marion and she's as cute as can be. They could give us some advice."

Dad looked up from his steak. "I don't think that's a good idea. We should be patient."

"But Bob! It's been five years! How much longer are we supposed to wait? All of our friends already have families!"

"I'm sure the doctors will figure something out, or nature will take its course."

Mom paused, biting her lower lip and turning her napkin ring over and over on the table.

"Will you at least have dinner with the Savages and meet darling Marion? You can see for yourself what an adopted child is like!"

Dad raised his eyes, his forehead wrinkling in waves, but nodded as he chewed.

Dr. Eric Savage was a respected physician, a considerate man, and an excellent sailor. Lillian Savage was a talented gardener and community volunteer. After conspiring with Mom, Mrs. Savage extended a gracious dinner invitation, and the four adults enjoyed cocktails and conversation in the large, elegant living room. French doors opened to gardens and the balmy summer evening, and water splashed lazily from a fountain. The air was fragrant with honeysuckle and roses, and light streamed into the room, low and golden. Three-year-old Marion toddled in on cue, a towheaded cherub with curly pigtails and pink cheeks. She wore a quilted robe covered with rosebuds, and slippers with tiny bells on the toes. She looked at Dad with her big blue eyes and thick lashes and climbed right into his lap, laying her head against his shoulder. Dad was so surprised he didn't know what to do. He awkwardly patted her arm as she nestled in and smiled out at the group.

"Well, Bob," Lillian laughed, "Marion certainly thinks you're something special!" And with that, Dad was ready to consider adoption and Mom's plan moved forward. They contacted the same agency the Savages used and began the process of paperwork, interviews, and home inspections.

The first child Mom and Dad adopted was my brother, Eric, named in honor of Dr. Savage. Eric was nine months old when placed with Mom and Dad, and they were thrilled with his quintessential Gerber baby face and chubby arms that reached for them. There was no discernable evidence of this little boy's loss and confusion after languishing in foster care for nine months. His biological mother wanted to keep him and hoped his father would return from military duty and marry her. She visited Eric often, sometimes bringing her mother, and they agonized over leaving him. They could see his placement wasn't easy. When Eric was four months old, his foster family moved out of state, and he was placed a second time, enduring another adjustment to new caregivers. When he was nine months old, his mother faced the harsh news that his father was a married man who had returned from service but never called her. Heartbroken, she finally signed her child's adoption papers.

Although this was done in Eric's "best interest," he could only experience his relinquishment as abandonment. He would develop feelings of being unwanted and unworthy, especially as he had already been handed to multiple sets of strangers. Eric's sense of value and trust had been deeply eroded by the time he came to our parents.

While these feelings are common in adoptees, they weren't documented or discussed in 1953, and Mom and Dad had no understanding of Eric's shock or grief. Nor did they give any recognition to the name he'd had for nine months. When he was handed over to this new family, his prior life was obliterated. In 1953 they believed eager parents were all he needed to be happy. They didn't recognize the intelligence of preverbal children, respect the attachments they had formed, or the identity they'd already claimed. There was no literature to describe the issues of separation and loss in adoption or warnings about the ensuing emotional and behavioral problems to which these children were prone.

In early childhood photos, Eric looks confused about the world around him. Home movies show him as a curious, hyperactive child, running around at fast-forward speed. Always in motion and easily frustrated, he often found his way into mischief, testing the patience of the adults around him. He certainly tried the patience of our mother. Luckily, Grandma and Grandpa Vincentz lived nearby and were happy to provide all the help Mom needed.

As it turned out, mothering was not a job Mom enjoyed. She wanted children to enhance her stature and reflect her achievements, but actual children interfered with her goals and focus. They smashed her sense of control and often mortified her. Still, Mom wanted to fit in with the 1950s American dream, and after adopting Eric, my parents kept their names on the list for additional children, eventually adopting four of us.

I arrived about a year after they adopted Eric. Mom and Dad were excited to receive a call that a baby girl was available and would be ready to be picked up in a couple of days. Though they were scheduled to visit Dad's good friend Hank and his wife, Ella, at the Jersey Shore that weekend, Mom didn't see why their plans had to change. They could swing by the adoption agency to pick me up on their way out of town. Now five weeks old, I had been in the hospital nursery, alone, for the first week of my life, then in foster care for a month. Mom wasn't focused on the needs of an infant coming into a new home. She was thinking more about the grand surprise I would be to Hank and Ella!

Mom and Dad arrived at their friends' home, the wheels of their car crunching over the gravel driveway. Ella emerged from the blue-shingled house, smiling brightly as she wiped her hands on a pretty apron, and dodging her young sons as they darted around her. The boys slammed their hands against the car windows and peered in, looking for toddler Eric.

"Mom!" cried Ella's youngest. "There's a little baby!"

Ella clapped her hands to her heart and ran to the car. Seeing me, she grabbed Mom, and they twirled around together and cried.

With no forewarning, Ella accommodated a baby as best she could. They didn't have a crib, so Hank cleared a bureau drawer for my bed, and Ella ran to find some formula so everyone could go about enjoying the summer fun they'd planned.

This was always the punchline of childhood stories I was told— they never let me interfere with other plans. Apparently, I was the child who adapted to their needs with the least resistance.

One evening, when I was eighteen months old, Mom and Dad hosted their weekly bridge group. They'd put me to bed in my crib and left the bureau lamp lit, dimmed with one of my little chiffon dresses draped over the shade. Mom closed my door and returned to the living room, where homemade cake and a percolator of coffee waited on the dining room table. The card table held a bowl of unshelled walnuts, a shiny silver nutcracker, and embroidered linen napkins. Their good friends gathered to enjoy one another's company and spirited competition, and, as always, the game was lively. Cards were slapped onto the table, friends shrieked with laughter and gasped with trumps.

That night, however, my crying interrupted their fun. As it became louder and more disruptive, Mom stood, slid the pocket door to the bedroom hallway closed, and returned to the card table, smoothing her velvet dress gracefully as she sat. When my cries became shrieks, my father got up to check on me. Down the hall, in the furthest bedroom, I was pressed against the back of my crib, red-faced and screaming, as the top of my bureau raged with flames. Dad moved quickly but calmly to put the fire out with glasses of water from the bathroom sink, and once he extinguished it, the adults returned to their bridge game, and, as the story goes, "a fun time was had by all."

I wasn't told what happened to me after the fire. Did I join the bridge party? Did someone hold me and comfort me while the game continued? Was I left to fall asleep with the chest of drawers dripping and smoke curling at the ceiling? The bureau's scorched top was later covered with an embroidered doily made by Grandma Vincentz and remained in my room for most of my childhood. I remember lifting the doily to stare at the dark, cracked surface, each time confused about why they would leave damaged furniture in my room. We didn't have damaged furniture anywhere else in the house. Didn't they care about my room? Wasn't my space important? How could they think a thin cloth was all they needed to hide the ugly, black-fissured burn marks?

CHAPTER THREE

A World as Big as All Alone
1964–1968

S hadow Lake almost touched the back of our redbrick ranch house, which sat in front of a steeply sloped yard. The living room had a large picture window facing the lake, and the yard fell away so abruptly it looked as if you were on the deck of a ship pushing through the water. Folds of sunlit waves moved across the lake, stirring light that rose and slid wrinkles across the ceiling.

In the spring, yellow ducklings appeared, bobbing through bright blue and white reflections, and a pair of swans returned every summer, gliding through the thick water stilled by the heat. We swam from the sandy beach Dad made for us and jumped off the white belly of our overturned wooden rowboat, *Moby Dick*. In the autumn, leaves turned golden and fell into the lake, lit by fiery sunsets as Canadian geese honked overhead in their perfect V formation. In the winter, we played ice hockey under rigged-up floodlights and had skating parties with girls who wore pretty hats and mittens. Cookies and thermoses of hot chocolate stood by on a sled.

Many winter days, Mom surprised us when we arrived home from school for our lunch hour, meeting us at the top of the driveway with those same thermoses filled with hot tomato soup. We'd rush to change out of our shoes and sidestep down to the lake in our skates. A few chugs from the red-plaid flasks and we were off! Grateful to have the wind in our faces after sitting in stuffy classrooms all morning, we flew across the ice!

Mom skated too, though I don't remember any other mothers being out there. Pushing away from the zigzag of children, she moved with confidence and control, zooming across the lake with strong, purposeful strides. There was a jaunty self-satisfaction in how she moved, standing tall as she kicked one leg out and crossed it in front of the other. Fragments of whatever song she was singing floated through the air, adding cadence to her long, graceful movements. Sometimes she would practice an arabesque, one leg raised high behind, her arms outstretched, gliding an impressive distance. Mom looked like a different person out on the ice, someone I didn't know. She was peaceful and at ease, and I often stopped to watch her in wonder.

These lunches ended in a mad dash when someone realized the time. We hurriedly changed back into our shoes at the top of the driveway, where the carpool picked us up for the return to school. I'd see Mom still out on the ice as we scrambled to leave, waving as she gathered speed and turned away.

Winter picnics were Mom's escape from the chore of having kids home for lunch, arranged more for her than for us. Skating was one of the ways she broke free of the dreary work of motherhood, as we saw in the home movies Dad took. One particular reel was filmed from the large picture window. Mom stepped cautiously down the backyard to the lake. When she skated out onto the ice, her arms spread wide, it was as if her heart lifted to the sky and every burden left her, vaporizing into the white, cold air above.

Dad shot hours of 8 mm home movies, and despite the lack of sound, they captured our family well. There is footage of a Christmas Eve where my beautiful mother, in a red dress and gold Christmas tree pin, is sitting in front of the fireplace with two freshly pajamaed toddlers. It's a struggle to keep the squirming children still as she reads from a tiny Bible, and each time a toddler bends to look up the chimney or touch the stockings behind them, they are pressed back into a seated position like dolls with bendable joints. Mom smiles gracefully at the camera and continues to read scriptures to the disinterested tots, adding exaggerated facial expressions for the soundless film. It's clear that Mom means to be the star of this Christmas Eve show, and her efforts for perfection missed the giddy joy her children felt in hanging their Christmas stockings and looking for Santa.

There are also lots of home movies of the summer weekends we spent camping with our motorboat. We loved that boat! Canvas tents were packed into the hull, along with red-plaid picnic coolers, green Coleman lanterns, and assorted groceries. Speeding through the open air, foam spraying up, hull smacking down, we raced over the waves, giggles bursting from our bellies with every bounce. I was always surprised to see the movies of Mom in a sailor's cap, sunglasses, and Bermuda shorts, seated in the back of the boat, legs outstretched on the bench. She was engrossed in a book but smiled at the camera momentarily before turning her attention back to its pages while her four children crawled precariously over the deck, squirming like puppies on the loose. Her head remained down, her focus unwavering from her reading.

But it's the waterskiing footage I think Mom was most proud of. Her athletic body looked great in a swimsuit, and she was happy, even somewhat cocky. Those sequences often showed Mom copying the daredevil aquatic stunts of various weekend guests.

Always determined to outshine everyone, Mom took her turn immediately after any guest performed something impressive. She showed laser focus as she began each trick, setting her face in deep concentration as she executed the maneuver. Once completed, she wiped the spray from her face with a that's-how-you-do-it-boys shake and leaned back on her skis, shoulders proud as she bounced across the water. She stole every scene.

Mom was an active, busy woman who always had something to do, somewhere to go. She led an engaging life filled with purpose, and even as a child, I understood that she was doing good things and others appreciated her efforts. She was a pillar of our church and served as interim minister after earning a master of divinity degree in her sixties. (That option hadn't been open to her as a young woman.) A perpetual student, Mom earned multiple advanced degrees, including a PhD in education, which she pursued when I was in high school. Throughout her life, education and women's issues were of prime importance to her, and she held leadership positions in charitable organizations on the local and national level.

Running a household with four children didn't interest Mom, especially as we grew up and became more emotionally demanding. When we were little, she was a distracted parent, but as we grew older, she was most often exasperated.

Raising children turned out to be complex and messy, with no recognition or guarantee of success. At least two of us were bona fide rebels: my older brother ran a mile a minute and always pushed boundaries, and my little sister possessed a soul filled with rage and fear. My younger brother initially wore leg braces and needed surgery, and Mom forever viewed him as vulnerable and weak. Of all my siblings, it was easiest for me to go along with the things she valued: I followed directions, was a good student, and was calm and malleable. While our behaviors were the textbook responses of adopted children, either testing their adopted family by acting out or giving in with total compliance, there weren't any such books available on raising adopted children at the time. Thus, mothering the four of us turned out to be incredibly confusing and disappointing for my success-driven mother.

Mom was not educated on the issues adoptees typically grapple with, such as anxieties over separation and loss, difficulties establishing trust or dealing with control, and fear of rejection. Nor was she aware of how these experiences often manifested as social, academic, or psychological problems. She didn't understand how difficult it was for an adoptee to accept love, given the indelible memory of abandonment. She never expected it would be so hard to parent adopted children, or that they would not eagerly soak up her love and guidance to become shining reflections of her values.

As we grew up and away from Mom's vision of a perfect family, she responded to the stress of parenting by distancing herself from it, seeking refuge in activities that enhanced her self-esteem. She had tremendous success dealing with people and problems outside of the home, where her efforts to help were seen as selfless and were deeply valued. The wider world held a generous view of her as loving and giving, but we didn't experience that as much at home.

I remember skating across the lake one winter's night, away from my brothers and their friends playing hockey in the floodlights. I was alone, gliding over smooth black ice, each stroke of my blades releasing the damp smell of lake water that rose for a moment, then shattered into the freezing air. I stopped and looked back at our house, its lights barely visible. The sky above was endless, filled with brilliant stars, and stretched beyond the boundaries of anything I could see, reaching places I couldn't imagine. The air was deeply cold, and voices bounced across the ice with a ghostly, hollow sound. My legs went weak as I pictured the blinding black water beneath me and the infinity above. I didn't know if I would make it back to the shore. I froze with the fear of how big the world was and how small I felt.

CHAPTER FOUR

Committing to Perfection

1967

When I was twelve, Mom was thrilled to accept a position at her alma mater as a mathematics instructor. She was an exemplary teacher, passionate about her work and often so immersed in her day she forgot to eat, sacrificing her lunch hour to help the throng of students waiting outside her office. It was almost dinnertime when her Buick Skylark bombed down our driveway and pulled in front of the garage. We knew she was home when we heard her car horn blaring, summoning one of us to open the door. My room was farthest from there, but as soon as I heard honking, I dropped my pencil, shoved my books aside, and ran. Racing toward the living room, I careened past the picture window, down the basement stairs, and into the cold garage, where grit pushed through my stocking feet and up between my toes. I threw open the door in a whirl of dust and dry leaves to see Mom's tense and angry face behind the headlights, the heel of her hand resting on the horn, ready to blow it again. It would've taken a lot less time for her to get out of the car and open the garage door herself; it wasn't very heavy. For whatever reason, she wouldn't do it.

It wasn't until many years later that I understood how exhausted Mom was when she arrived home, how much she hated cooking, and how deeply she resented preparing meals for the family. Sitting down for dinner was a sacred ritual in our house, so I never imagined she dreaded it. We ate promptly at 6:30. No excuses. We sang the blessing with our heads bowed; the table was dressed with good linens, engraved silver napkin rings, and candles. While the setting was lovely, the food was awful. Shriveled baked potatoes, frozen steak thawed and cooked in an electric skillet, iceberg lettuce wedges with bottled dressing, and canned applesauce. I didn't know that in some homes, food was prepared with joy and received and savored with gratitude. In our house, dinner was something you got through.

My job was to set the table, and Mom was very particular about how it should be cleared. A large round aluminum tray was stashed next to the breakfront, and Mom would snap at me if I carried items to the kitchen without including them on a fully loaded tray. "Janet, that's not efficient! I hate wasted effort! Fill the tray up before you bring anything into the kitchen!"

Why she cared if I took one or a hundred trips puzzled me until I realized the longer I took, the more time she had to spend in the kitchen. We cleaned up leftovers and put things away while Dad stood at the sink, rinsing dishes in scalding water before placing them in the dishwasher. Tired and agitated, Mom moved quickly, with focused determination, like a runner summoning every ounce of strength to make it over the finish line. No one talked. It was such a relief when we could finally leave the kitchen. Mom hit the light switch hard as we walked out as if to say, *Okay, goddammit, I made it through again.*

Mom's moods from exhaustion and disappointment were pervasive. Most of the time her lips were set in a thin, tight line as she moved around the house shaking her head, muttering, and slamming things. She yelled all the time, not just in bursts of anger but with never-ending tirades during which she claimed to be the victim of ungrateful, selfish behavior. While her anger was not usually directed at me, witnessing it frightened me. I worried that our tenuous, disconnected family would implode.

She had a particularly tough time parenting my older brother, Eric. He didn't like school, couldn't sit still or focus, didn't stick with anything, and acted out. Parenting Eric was "baptism by fire" for her, and his rebellious teen years pushed her to the limit. His hair was too long, his pants too short, he got caught drinking beer, and was one of only a handful of students not going to a four-year college. Mom once turned to a close friend and said, "Well, at least we can take comfort in knowing that he's not really ours."

Her words shocked me. How easy would it be for her to abandon us just like our biological mothers did? Why *had* our birth mothers given us away?

Because a "good" mother wouldn't give a baby away, I pictured my birth mother as a fifteen-year-old streetwalker who wore Daisy Duke shorts and a midriff-baring top as she roamed up and down the nearby commuter highway. In my mind, she had remained fifteen for the rest of her life because that explained why she hadn't kept me. I didn't want to think of her as a responsible adult; that was too painful a rejection. And even as a child I never bought into the idea that my birth mother gave me away because she loved me and it was in my best interest. She *loved* me but *abandoned* me? That was beyond my comprehension.

My self-image became that of a trashy teenage streetwalker's discarded baby. I was lucky anyone wanted me—lucky to have a home at all. I resolved to be the perfect adopted daughter and earn my place at the table in my borrowed home. I would look and behave the right way and achieve all the right things. I couldn't risk any other path. After all, my life in the redbrick house with my adopted family wasn't awful. While I don't ever remember being hugged by Mom, and she rarely expressed love or approval, she wasn't hurting me in any way I could identify. She yelled a lot, but not at me. She was a good person who did so much for others. Unable to correlate the beloved teacher and volunteer with the angry, self-centered woman I knew, I believed the wider world's opinion of her and decided something was wrong with me. I just needed to adjust my expectations and work harder to make her happy. Mom *must be* a good mother because she dedicated herself to the service of others and adopted four children. People told me how she saved their lives and was a loving and generous friend/mentor/colleague. She was an exemplary woman. We had a fine home and a nice life. So, why didn't I feel safe and connected with this mother?

I remember standing at the end of our front walk at night; the woods across the street were dark and hard. All their color was folded up deep within, their long shadows spread across the lawn. Behind me, the lights of the house felt distant and small. I didn't find comfort there, though I couldn't tell you why. A whiff of wood smoke drifted through the night air, dampness curled against my legs, and the mineral tang of cold stone rose into my throat. I arched my neck and looked up. Bare trees towered above me, poking into the deep dome of sky; white stars smeared high above. My eyes remained with the heavens as deeper and deeper layers revealed themselves, until I was frightened by how far away they were and felt the mind-boggling enormity of the universe swallowing me up. I watched the stars and thought about the world they stretched over and wondered if it felt safer somewhere else.

CHAPTER FIVE

My Refuge in the Storm
1964

My father was my salvation, and I adored him. He was quiet while Mom was loud, patient when she was not, and generous in every way. He had a dry sense of humor, a twinkle in his eye, and he made me laugh every day! He wasn't confrontational but knew how to get his way if something was important. He never raised his voice or said unkind things, though I knew there were people he didn't like. He was my hope and inspiration and taught me by example.

One day, I was emptying the dishwasher during one of Mom's tirades. She yelled, slammed doors, flung cupboards open, threw books down, and yanked faucets on and off while ranting about whatever had upset her. I lifted glasses out of the blue plastic racks of the dishwasher, the sharp scent of detergent rising with the warm, moist air. I tried to distract myself by slowly and precisely lining them up in the maple cupboards and contemplating how long the brown plaid Con-Tact paper had been on the shelves. Grabbing another glass, a trickle of soapy water ran down my thumb and Mom's ranting intruded again, her volume a few notches higher than earlier. Every part of me tensed. No focus on dishes could keep it at bay. It was the same every time she lost her temper. She made her point over and over and over, escalating until it exhausted us. Her tirades were vicious, circular, and pointless. How could my intelligent, sane, in-control mother indulge in such out-of-control, crazy, stupid behavior? Nothing about it made sense. It was torturous. I shrank with her rants, curling into myself, trying to escape.

That particular day, instead of folding in, I got mad. Anger shot through me—I couldn't take it anymore! There were five other people in our house, and none of us behaved the way she did, nor had we done anything to deserve such unmitigated wrath. It *had* to stop. *She* had to stop. With the glass still in hand, I rushed out of the kitchen toward Mom's voice and considered smashing the glass at her feet, commanding her to shut up, stopping her in her tracks. Pulling my arm back, preparing to throw the glass, I looked around the living room—where was she?

My father was reading the *New York Times* in his green easy chair. He was always reading the *Times*. He read it cover-to-cover every day, which is why he knew something about everything. Dad could talk about any subject, and I learned something new whenever I asked him about schoolwork. He was also genuinely interested in my thoughts and answered my questions with patience and humor. That day, as he sat there, tuning my mother out, immersed in reading while she carried on and on, I saw a choice. It wasn't necessary to escalate an impossible situation and resort to smashing glasses and raising voices. There was another way to handle this, and I was looking at the example—I could be like my father, invoking calm, quiet, and distance. It didn't occur to me to question why he remained passive and never interceded. She was a hurricane, a force of nature, and her anger overwhelmed all of us, including him.

Watching how he managed himself brought great relief and reminded me there was a benefit to not sharing blood with my mother: her DNA didn't define me, and my behavior didn't have to mirror hers. I could choose who to pattern myself after. It shocked me when my mother said she was relieved my brother wasn't really theirs, but now I was relieved I wasn't really hers. I could choose to pattern myself after my father. A feeling of peace and control flooded through me, and lowering my hand, I walked back to the kitchen. My decision was conscious and deliberate. I remember the moment as if it were yesterday. It was the first time I realized I could shape myself and build something inside the big, black void instead of constantly feeling helpless and scared. Of course, I was still young, and that was easier said than done, but I had seen the possibility and tucked it away in the back of my mind.

Dad's way of doing things was always better than Mom's. When in charge of bedtime, his strategy was to pull out his fiddle and dance us into exhaustion, playing back-to-back jigs like "The Irish Washerwoman" and "Turkey in the Straw" until we danced ourselves silly. With our arms flung wide, we spun in crazy circles, giggling as we smashed into each other, the room tilting and twirling. We ran up and down the burgundy horsehair sofa, its twisted silk fringe shaking like a hula skirt. We dropped off the backs of chairs and rolled onto the gray pile carpet and under the piano bench. We sent the blue damask drapes sailing as we pranced behind them, beating back their heavy cover with whirling hands. Dad played until we dropped in place. Then he picked us up one by one and deposited us in our beds.

Fiddle, mandolin, piano, organ, church choir, my father loved music. He played our piano every evening, and one of his favorite pieces was Rachmaninoff's "Prelude in C-Sharp Minor." It begins with three long, low, descending octaves before they alternate with complex passages and finally burst into a frenzy. It is breathtaking and mesmerizing. When I was five, Dad showed me how to play the three opening notes, which we referred to as the "bong, bong, bong" notes. I stood at the keyboard and used both hands to punch out the three opening octaves. They reverberated through my body, and I could feel the excitement of what was to come. Dad moved his large hands over the keys, deftly playing the musical response, until a nod signaled me to sound one of the octaves again, and he followed with another complex passage. When the octaves came faster than I could handle them I'd climb onto the bench next to him and watch in awe as his hands moved faster and faster. So many notes, so much sound, so fast, so complicated! I wondered how a brain could manage all of it and was so proud of my father. Being part of that incredible music, something he cherished, made me feel honored and special. Years later, I learned to play Rachmaninoff's "Prelude in C-Sharp Minor," and although I can only manage half of it, executing any small part of it brings his love back into the room.

While Dad wasn't the flower gardener Grandma Leef was, he'd inherited her love of growing things and creating beautiful outdoor spaces. He loved working in the yard creating rock gardens and building stone walls for our driveway. I watched him trudge wheelbarrows of sand up and down the hill to create a beach at the edge of Shadow Lake. Our front lawn was always green, and where it was too shady for grass, he planted thousands of pachysandra plants. There was always a lot of shade because my father loved trees.

I spent my Saturdays following him around the property. He dug a small garden for me to plant and always included me on his run for supplies. The feed store was one of my favorite destinations. My nose tickled with the first acrid bite of stacked fertilizer, and I can still see the exact toast color of the wood floors, dusty with sawdust and discarded receipts. It was as quiet as a library, with only the occasional muffled conversation in an aisle and, every now and then, the sparkly ring of the cash register. Standing at the tall racks of seed packets, I studied their colorful illustrations. Allowed to choose as many as my heart desired, I did so based solely on how pretty the picture was. Dad looked them over and told me which ones would grow in our yard, before I spread the smooth, shiny envelopes across the counter as proudly as a winning poker hand, imagining the fairy-tale garden I'd create.

I spent hours in my little plot, planting and watering, while my father worked nearby on his projects, the sweet smell of his pipe or cigar drifting through the air. He claimed the smoke kept mosquitoes away. You could always find pouches of cherry pipe tobacco on his workbench, along with glossy cigar boxes, which, once empty, were used to hold treasures of all sorts.

One year, Dad built multitiered rock walls on the far side of the house and told me I could design gardens there. White dogwood trees dotted the bordering woods, and a tall old tulip tree framed the lakeside. The ground was thick with moss, and only woodland plants would thrive in the deep shade, so we dug mature ferns from the woods across the street and transplanted violets and lily of the valley from the front yard rock garden. I fussed over the placement of each one, stepping back and adjusting until it was perfect. We also borrowed a white wrought iron bench from the front yard. It was beautiful against the deep green shade and created a lovely place to rest in my little secret garden. It was more personal and private than my bedroom. No one else cared about that hidden shady spot, but it was a sanctuary for me.

I wanted to photograph my garden to capture every detail, every leaf and blossom. Propping my elbows on the uneven rock wall I leaned into a violet with my Instamatic camera, centering the smallest botanical detail in the viewfinder. When the film came back, I was shocked to find the image blurred beyond recognition. To this day, every time I bend to take a close-up of a flower, I remember that deep purple violet with its bright green heart-shaped leaves. I smell the damp earth and the cold minerals of the rock walls. I see the dappled shade and soft filtered light. In that vivid memory, I feel Dad's love and remember how safe I felt in that space. Sitting there I had a sense of finding myself, of the possibility that one day I would feel a solid core and a connection to this earth. Deep down I recognized that had something to do with learning to be comfortable alone, delving within, and experiencing the solace of the natural world.

Taking that close-up photo was also one of the first times I remember trying to capture a specific image, of framing an object the way I wanted to present it. It was the beginning of my interest in art. I had recently started playing with watercolor and oil paints as well as photography. I was devastated when my photo failed and decided it was more reliable to create images myself, so I focused on painting, which soon became a defining activity of my childhood and a major area of my studies in college.

The memory of that day in my garden is a touchstone not only for the arc of my life and my artistic journey but, most importantly, for the memory of my father, who truly saw and encouraged me.

In elementary school, one of my best friends, Susan, lived across the street from a little brook that ran through a pretty dell. That small woodland was a magic garden filled with dogwood trees, mountain laurel, Queen Anne's lace, wild iris, forget-me-nots, ferns of every sort, and large pillows of moss. Susan and I loved to play there, floating blocks of discarded wood down the stream, pretending they were racehorses. As the brook swirled around rocks, Susan and I moved to make foaming eddies, fast whirlpools, and wide-open chutes. Then we'd watch as our wood horses bobbed and spun their way through every challenge. We constructed fairy-size stalls for our horses at the streamside, using beds of moss and canopies of ferns, leaves, and flowers.

It was the best place to be one hot and muggy summer day—the kind when the heat breaks only with a thunderstorm. Cool water curled against my knees and dripped down my wrists as I guided my pretend horse through the current. The damp moss along the stream smelled like the woods in spring, and the sound of bubbling water tickled my ears and lulled my brain. I was lost in play with no sense of the world around me.

At the end of one race, I grabbed my "horse" and glanced up at the sky. The light had dimmed, and clouds were forming into towering mounds of deep lavender with glowing white-hot edges. Beams of gold shot through them toward earth, splitting and spreading wider and wider until they dissolved into blue dust at the horizon. It was something I'd seen only in religious paintings, never in the real world, and I was transfixed and terrified at the same time. I imagined it was a biblical sign. Those golden shafts looked like heaven opening with paths for the angels to descend. I didn't think mortals were supposed to see something so holy. Why was I seeing this? Was I about to go to heaven? Was I going to die? My anxiety exploded and I dropped my soggy wood horse and ran out of the dell as fast as I could.

Heart pounding, sandals slapping, I raced home without looking up and ran inside, gasping for breath. I peered cautiously through our picture window, only to find that there was nothing left to see. Within just a few minutes, the clouds had come together. They were now flat and dull, their light an ordinary gray. I had imagined horns and harps, organs and angels, and imminent death, but now, panting, sweat dappled, and confused, I stared across the lake toward the setting sun.

Dad appeared in the living room, newspaper tucked under his arm, and looked at the breathless, disheveled me. I turned to him, still shaken and unsure. "Dad, do you believe in heaven?"

My father was a man who went to church every Sunday, who never missed choir, who played hymns at home on the piano. He would know about heaven, and he'd help me understand what I had just seen. He paused and looked down at me with a smile. He patted my head.

"I believe heaven is the feeling you leave in other people while you're still here on this earth." He smiled at me, then continued to his chair and opened the newspaper.

I'll never forget what he said. His answer felt so grown-up and perfectly described how he lived his life. I studied my father in that moment. Though he was simply reading the *New York Times* in his big green chair, there was such grace about him, such conviction. The room was quiet, with only my labored breathing and the occasional crinkling of Dad's paper. Gently, I started to settle. My stomach slipped back into place, my breathing slowed, and everything eased. No longer afraid of angels descending to earth on beams of light and carting me off to heaven, I understood I'd seen something extraordinarily beautiful, but it wasn't heaven. Heaven was already here on earth. It was how you treated others. It was love and respect as true as my father's.

CHAPTER SIX

Downhill from Here
1966

My parents loved to ski, and every winter weekend we drove three hours to Pine Hill, New York, on twisting, nausea-inducing back roads. Luckily, I usually slept through the drive, but the arrival was always abrupt. The overhead light flicked on, the car doors flew open, and frigid air blasted me awake. I climbed out into the clear, still night, sharp with pine pitch, and the ice-blue snow squeaked under my feet as I slipped along the walkway into the strange house where we rented rooms for the season. Everything about the house frightened me.

Henry Morton, the elderly owner, was cadaverous. He towered over us, his white head reaching close to the high ceilings, his corduroy pants baggy and worn. He was never happy with our interruption of his evening but tolerated us for the needed income and, though I doubt he would admit it, the few days of company we provided.

We arrived late and went directly to bed. The room we kids slept in had arched windows with heavy molding, and the streetlight outside the bay window cast a grimy yellow glow over the thick paint. Lumpy mattresses outfitted the curved iron bedframes, but at least the linens smelled fresh and clean. After I climbed into bed in the dark, my parents would lift the down comforter high above me and let it float gently over me, embracing every curve of my body with its warmth as it landed. I'd burrow in and drift off to sleep.

By the light of day, you could see that Henry Morton's home was wedged against the base of a steep, pine-covered hill. The only thing between the house and those impenetrable dark woods was an ice-covered river. I hated the way the hills in the valley folded in on one another like hands cupped over my mouth, and I itched to be on our way up to the slopes. It was such a relief to reach the summit and breathe in the crystalline air. The morning sun reached over my shoulder to the low hills across the valley and caught on windows of distant homes, gold and gleaming, while broad fields were randomly bathed in light or cast into shadow.

My skis flew as I shot down the slopes, muscles tensed, speed rising in my stomach, frigid air stinging my cheeks. Nothing lay ahead but the white, open run. I had a sense of freedom and control—a feeling of being strong and in command. It felt good. Usually meek and unsure of myself, skiing surprised me with a power I didn't recognize but liked. Unfortunately, I couldn't pull that intensity into my everyday life. Moments like bombing down the mountain were anomalies to me. In my mind, I was weak, always less-than, forever an empty center where nothing held.

The bottom of the mountain was everything I didn't like about skiing: the crowds, the lines, and the busy lodge where my family met for lunch. We didn't eat in the log-beamed cafeteria. Instead, Mom brought picnic lunches in waxed paper packets—Wonder Bread smeared and stained with peanut butter and jelly. The sandwiches were invariably squashed beneath the oranges that needed peeling, their thick, yellow rind sticking under my fingernails. We sat sideways or backward on picnic table benches and ate in silence. I envied the families around us enjoying crispy french fries and steaming hot chocolate from trays, talking and laughing with one another while my family was simply refueling.

One day after lunch, when I was twelve, Mom and I decided to ski together—a rare occurrence. As the afternoon unfolded, I enjoyed it more and more. We were outside and active, the best scenario for spending time with Mom, and the day was bright with fresh powder. We skied gracefully and talked as we rode the chair lift. Everything was ordinary in the best of ways. I was grateful for Mom's company and raised my face to the warming sun with a sense of pride and belonging.

During one run, we paused halfway down to catch our breath, stopping on the side of the slope where the woods were heavy with snow, and tangled branches stood white against the deep green pines. It was peaceful and warm with that thick blanket of powder over everything, like a down comforter. We chatted as we rested, talking about the beautiful Christmas gifts we'd recently received, the fluffy blue angora sweater Mom wore and the classic cable sweater I had on, both knit for us by Grandma Leef. Ready to move on, we arranged our poles back onto our hands and stomped clumps of snow from our skis when Mom said, "I've always been grateful that Grandma Leef treated you kids like you were real grandchildren." Then she pushed off and headed down the mountain, singing aloud as she went. I stopped short, instantly stung. *What? What did she say? Did my mother really just say, "like real grandchildren"?* I was stunned.

Why would she ever say that to me? Why *wouldn't* we be thought of as real grandchildren? Since I didn't have any concept of my heritage or bloodline, I had no idea why our grandparents might not see us as regular grandchildren. Despite my own feelings of disconnection, which I felt but didn't understand, it never occurred to me that others might feel that way toward us, especially our loving grandparents. I always thought it was just me who felt disconnected because something was wrong inside me. Was it actually something they felt too? Were my worst fears true? That we didn't belong? That we weren't really a part of our borrowed family? That they saw us as outliers? I watched Mom glide down the mountain. She looked so relaxed and happy, as if she didn't have a care in the world, while I stood shocked by her revelation of the truth: I was not her real child, I didn't belong, and she was surprised when anyone treated me as if I did.

CHAPTER SEVEN

Deathly Fears

1965

Grandma Leef lived in Minnesota, and we called her Big Grandma. She was tall and commanding with a hearty laugh, impeccable taste, and a beautiful home. Big Grandma had an unerring eye for color and dazzling gardens. Lush borders of blue delphiniums, pink roses, and prized dahlias framed the yard, while smaller beds were tangled with juicy strawberries and raspberries, perfect for her homemade shortcake—Dad's favorite. Grandma's home had pale blue walls and gold-framed paintings. I especially loved the one of a pink sun rising over the snow-covered lakes of her Scandinavian homeland. Her guest bath displayed hand lotion made with rose petals, its scent as genuine as the perfectly opened roses in her garden. She served every meal with her good china, her silverware gleaming in the bright Midwestern light as she told us to "Use your good things every day!"

Although we saw her only once a year on summer vacation, I liked Big Grandma and felt comfortable in her lovely, sun-filled home. It was peaceful, organized, and clean, with modern furniture and hand-woven rugs. Grandma was a Master Weaver and an accomplished needlework artist. Her sunroom held multiple looms and shelves filled with yarn of every color, spools and bolts all creating a pretty patchwork. Just outside on the patio, overlooking the garden, was a double-sided glider with a bright, striped canopy trimmed with pom-poms. I loved the dreamy, sleepy way its motion made me feel.

I had six girl cousins in Minnesota and looked forward to our time together every summer. We swam in the clear turquoise water of their country club pool and sipped icy Cokes on the hot cement deck as our water shadows evaporated. We played with Barbie dolls and had sleepovers, and when our families drove to Grandma's lake cabin, we paddled canoes to the far reaches of the lake, daring one another to go further despite wildly exaggerated stories of danger. It was even better when our California cousins also visited Minnesota—three more girl cousins! Giggling with anticipation, quarters jingling in our pockets, we'd walk through the birch woods to the local canteen to buy pop and listen to the jukebox. I felt so cool and grown up and loved being with all of them. Studying each of them like an admiring little sister, noting their hair and fashion choices, I also noticed how they matched their parents. Each looked like their father or mother, and a few looked most like Grandma Leef! I could see the threads binding this family together—physical appearance, gestures, humor, tastes—and anyone could have identified them as part of the same clan. They all fit into the puzzle in a way I did not. They shared blood, but I didn't. I was not *really* a Leef cousin, after all. Still, I liked this family. This was a perfectly fine family to belong to.

Back in New Jersey, my mother's mother, Grandma Vincentz, was affectionately called Little Grandma. When she gathered me in her arms for warm, mushy hugs, she was a source of comfort and ease in my childhood, although I was embarrassed by how fat and sloppy she was. Her house was dark and musty but filled with intriguing things. Every drawer, cupboard, and tabletop held bowls of curious stuff, though many of her things were made in Japan or were broken. The rooms appeared all shadows and corners, and the old furniture smelled faintly of propane and liver. Grandma crocheted doilies that covered every surface, held stains from random cups of tea, and collected crumbs in their lacey threads. She cooked crepes for lunch, drenched in butter and warm maple syrup, and made delicious rice pudding every Sunday, creamy with sweet custard and a hint of cinnamon. She let us run and play anywhere we wanted, rarely said no, and always took our side in any disagreement with our parents. There were no expectations, no pretenses with Grandma Vincentz—just love.

Mom was much younger than her brothers, and our New Jersey cousins were much older than us. Though we spent major holidays together, they felt more like family friends. I could see the physical resemblance among the Vincentz clan but didn't think of them as my relatives. Grandma wasn't as close to her sons as she was with Mom, and those young adult cousins weren't around much. My siblings and I were lucky to have Little Grandma to ourselves.

She was around most days after school, especially once Mom returned to teaching when I was in middle school. At that age I wanted personal space and wasn't always as happy to have her there as I was when I was little. With Mom teaching and my brothers at sports practice, she was the only intrusion on my afternoon. I'd hope and pray I'd have the place to myself as I walked home from school. Holding my breath as I neared the bend in our street, my next few steps would reveal whether I had my freedom for a few hours or not. I'd shut my eyes and wish that Grandma's car wasn't in the driveway, but it usually was. One day as I approached, there she stood over a flock of shopping bags in the trunk.

Hearing her cheery, "Well, hello, Missy. How are you today?" instantly irritated the adolescent me. I walked grudgingly to her car and looked away as she picked through the bags, putting the most dented cans aside for herself. Grandma shopped every day for anything on sale or for something she could get the manager to mark down, thus we ended up with too many cans of dented applesauce and tomato soup. I carried one load of bags to the house and returned for a second to find her unraveling a wad of damp newspapers filled with masses of lilacs. She stood behind her car, unwrapping bundle after bundle until the trunk was filled with blooms, then pulled the wild branches to her chest and turned to me. "That's all, Missy. Thanks for helping your old Grandma."

As we walked toward the house, she grabbed my arm to steady herself. I didn't like the touch of her soft, old flesh and was glad to release it once safely inside. She went straight to work on the lilacs, unhooking the tangled branches and jabbing them into every vase we owned. When they were full, she reached for empty applesauce and mayonnaise jars and filled them too. They were wild, unstudied, and loose, looking like they didn't care. She placed masses throughout the house, and I loved their redolent scent and how alive they made our home feel. In spite of my petulance, I was always grateful to Grandma for bringing the lilacs from her yard.

Once every branch was set, she returned to the kitchen and began rummaging through the refrigerator. "How about something nice to eat, Missy? Shall I fix you a little snack?"

"I'm not hungry."

"Did you learn a lot in school today?"

"No."

"That's nice."

Grandma focused on food more than anything else and loved being in the kitchen stirring, chopping, and slurping. Some of everything she got her hands on went into her mouth—a spoonful of still-liquid Jell-O, bread crusts, meat gnawed off leftover chicken bones. I loved my grandmother but hated both how she ate and her obsession with food. I avoided her in the kitchen as much as possible.

That day I found the peace and privacy I'd sought in my room. A large bunch of lilacs perfumed the air, and I lay down and watched sunlight glance off the white eyelet of my bedspread, breathing in the scent until I drifted off.

A knock on my door woke me, and Grandma waded in. Annoyed, I sat up grudgingly and looked at her with narrowed eyes.

"Here, Missy, buy yourself a little treat." She poked a dollar bill into my hand.

I stared at the damp dollar and felt awful. Her kindness called out my snippy adolescent behavior.

A few minutes later, I heard the mailman arrive, which offered me an excuse to follow her to the living room. I waited a few minutes for effect, then sauntered down the hall.

Grandma sat on the piano bench staring into the air, clutching a letter. Tears streamed down her face, glistening on stray whiskers, and running through the furrows of her plump skin. I'd never seen her cry before. I don't think I'd seen any adult cry before.

"What's the matter, Grandma?"

There was a long pause before she whispered, "My old friend Pearl died."

I didn't know Pearl or anything about her, and I didn't know what to say. Mortified to think how rude I'd been, I froze as she slumped on the piano bench, her multiple chins meeting the folds of her stomach. Her grief shocked me. It felt so private. Edging back to my room, I sat and watched shadows slide across the wall. It was late afternoon, and my room felt small and suffocating, as if I were jammed inside. When a door closed and I heard footsteps outside, I climbed up to my window and watched as she got into her car and drove away.

Tiptoeing back to the living room, I peered out the front door to the empty street where her car had been parked. The house was still, and dust turned in the shafts of sunlight streaming through the big picture window. Even there, in that large room, I felt something pressing in on me. It felt like the air had been sucked out of the room, and only grief remained.

The concept of death knocked me off my feet. It was the ultimate abandonment and loss—alone for eternity in a coffin underground, blank, black, forever. I was empty and lonely in life; the mind-boggling idea of feeling that way forever overwhelmed me. The fact that I wouldn't be conscious after death didn't occur to me. When I pictured eternal separation, rational thought was obliterated. It was an idea too painful to tolerate.

Thinking about dying magnified every isolated, abandoned feeling I held, but I also didn't want to die before I had an opportunity to "fix" myself—to repair the big black hole at my center. As long as I was alive, there was hope I could fill the void and find relief. I wanted to find peace, to feel whole and complete.

While many adolescents struggle with the idea of death, I never knew that adoptees often suffer intensely with it. Though some hazy, hidden part of me understood a connection between my sense of abandonment and my acute fear of dying, without concrete knowledge of the associations I couldn't understand or confront the issues they presented. I remained helpless in the face of devastating anxiety and vigilantly tried to protect myself from any risk of mortality, which included trying to avoid the massive panic attacks I believed could kill me.

My irrational fears couldn't be soothed in any way I knew of, not even through a heavy dependence on my adoptive parents. Though I was attached to them, we were not bonded—a distinction I felt but didn't understand at the time. We didn't share the complex biological and emotional connections a baby experiences when it bonds with its mother in utero, which are critical to a newborn's sense of wholeness and security.

I'd been untethered at birth and found that feeling more and more intolerable as I grew up. Although I didn't feel rooted with my adoptive parents, I depended on them and struggled with separation anxiety, which embarrassed me. Adoptees find it difficult to trust the permanence of their adoptive family. It doesn't feel solid, and they worry it will disappear. My reaction to that insecurity was to latch on to whatever was there. It was all I had. And while my adoptive parents did provide a home for me, I needed something they could never give me: a grounding sense of wholeness, of completion, of identity. I imagined those things would allow me to feel safe. I believed they would calm my fears and let me live as normal a life as my peers appeared to be enjoying.

CHAPTER EIGHT

A Plague of Anxiety

1966

When my sixth-grade Girl Scout troop planned a weekend trip to Williamsburg, Virginia, about a seven-hour drive from home, my disproportionate, age-inappropriate separation anxiety caused a terrifying, life-altering event.

Williamsburg is a fully restored colonial town and a popular vacation destination. The buildings are historically correct, the gardens stunning, and visitors watch blacksmiths and bakers in period costumes reenact every aspect of colonial life. Though I'd always wanted to see Williamsburg, I didn't want to go on this trip—I was afraid to travel so far from home.

I didn't mention the trip to my parents and told my troop leader I couldn't go. But I later heard my troop leader refer to it while chatting with Mom at church. Surprised to hear about the excursion for the first time, Mom assured her I certainly would be going, and later asked me why I hadn't mentioned it earlier. My heart dropped. I was embarrassed to tell her I was afraid to go and knew she'd be mortified if I were the only scout not participating. Too timid to make my true feelings known, I agreed to go. On departure day, I stood in the bus line as scared and shaky as a child going off to their first day of kindergarten. I told myself it would be alright. I'd get through it and maybe even have some fun.

After the long bus ride to Virginia, we settled into our motel, four girls to a room. Our leader checked on us, said goodnight, and turned the lights off as she shut the door. In the sudden pitch black, a ray of blue light from the parking lot slashed across the room. My eyes held on to that light as I tried to orient myself in the strange space with a door that opened to a sidewalk and with girls I didn't know well. As I lay there in the dark, a chill rolled up my spine and grabbed at my chest. The others were relaxed, chatting, and giggling as their conversation hopped from one topic to the next, eventually landing on religion. We were all from different Christian churches in the same small town, so the comments were agreeable and unremarkable, until one of the girls said, "You know, God is always watching over us. He is around all the time and sees everything you do. He is in this very room, here with us, watching us right now."

The image of a strange ghostly man loomed before me—a man formed of blue light hanging in the high corner of the room as if on a crucifix. His lifeless arms spread wide; his hollow body vibrated with an alien, neon glow; his head bowed as he glared down at us with soulless eyes. I buried my head in my pillow, my heart swooping in every direction, but the image wouldn't leave my mind. Within minutes I couldn't catch my breath and was shaking violently. Everything around me looked oddly far away as if I were peering through the wrong end of a telescope, and I was convinced I was dying far from my home and parents.

At some point a troop leader appeared at my bedside. Had the others noticed my panic? Did I say something to the girls? There is a length of time I don't remember at all. The troop leader sat at the edge of my bed, assuring me that I was alright, but I knew I wasn't, and her patronizing words made me feel foolish. Finally, I exhausted myself and fell into a deep sleep.

My memories of Williamsburg are vague, but I do remember walking its cobblestone streets tense and cautious, alert for the first sign of trouble in my brain. I was mortified by what had happened and didn't want to experience it again, whatever it had been. Was I going crazy? Remaining alert for signs of terror while trying to act like an ordinary, carefree schoolgirl was exhausting. I envied the other girls: present, engaged, light, and having so much fun.

Arriving home on Sunday evening was a relief. I thought I'd finally be safe. Instead, two days of holding myself together had worn me down, and I imploded.

The TV cart was wheeled into Mom's study, and I settled in with my brothers to watch our usual Sunday night program, *Disney's Wonderful World of Color.* The darkened room was stuffy and the nubby brown tweed on the couch scratched my thighs, but I was happy to get cozy in such a familiar place. My younger brother, Mark, curled into one corner of the sofa, and my older brother, Eric, sprawled out on the floor as the TV sputtered its hypnotic light in our direction. Mom was putting Susie to bed, and Dad sat in the living room reading the *New York Times.* Everything was calm and routine as Tinkerbell flew across the screen and tapped her magic wand to start the show, but suddenly I didn't feel well. The warm, dark study closed in, nausea churned, and a chill snaked through me. I felt weak and clammy as I stood to leave, and my heart raced as I floated through the house in a powdery haze. When I got to my room and flicked on the fluorescent lights, something inside me burst.

I sat on the edge of my bed shaking violently. I was too weak to stand but didn't want to lie down because I was afraid I'd picture myself dead. I don't remember calling my parents, but they were there, and though they stood next to me, they appeared eons away. Something had overtaken me. I watched them fade into dust and reappear like specters. They reached out to touch me, but I couldn't feel my body. A centrifuge kept spinning me apart. I was light flung into a whirlpool. My hands were mere particles evaporating into nothing. I tried to touch my head, but all I could feel was the voltage and tingling of millions of nerves. It was as if they were scattering into space, blowing away. I saw my parents' exchanged looks, the quick pace of their movements, their worry. They took turns sitting with me, never leaving me alone for a moment. The flick of a heel, the flap of a skirt out my door, and the brown wing-tip planted over the threshold—the changing of the guard until the doctor came.

I believed I was witnessing my own death and thought it was cruel to experience myself disintegrating, aware that I was about to be alone for eternity. Our family doctor, who in those days made house calls, said I was not dying, but beyond that I'm not sure he knew what he was looking at. Would he have known what a panic attack was? (Did people use the term "panic attack" then?) Were my parents given any explanation for my bizarre symptoms? If there was such an explanation, no one told me.

From that day on, rogue waves of terror plagued me for years. I never saw them coming. Each time another hit, I felt more tentative and worthless, vacant and illusory in both body and mind. In those horrible moments there was nothing solid or real anywhere within me. Any sense of myself disappeared. I wondered if having a connection to something tangible could stave off my mind-boggling fears of the unknown. Maybe if I shared biology with someone who'd had the same experience and could reassure me, or if I could see myself as part of a solid lineage with physical roots, I wouldn't fear evaporating into thin air—simply disappearing without a trace.

At first, my panic attacks frightened and confused my parents, but after I survived several, Mom and Dad seemed to think of them more as an annoyance than an emergency. They hoped the attacks would go away as suddenly as they'd appeared or stop if they ignored them. I know it was especially difficult for my mother to see me falling apart. I was the good child who never had problems, the good student, a polite and acceptable child—the best reflection of herself. She was determined to remove any shortcomings that might be developing. She had a solution, and it was God. I'd be okay if I had faith and turned all my "uncomfortable feelings" over to Him.

She told me this as we walked the footpath along the Boulevard one Sunday afternoon. I stared at my feet, kicking pebbles along the rough gray asphalt, and carried a single autumn daisy I'd picked from my garden; its bright white petals bobbed in and out of my view as my hand swung back and forth. Our steps crunched through piles of dried brown leaves, and the warm afternoon smelled of bonfires. There were enough peaceful moments as we walked that I imagined Mom as sympathetic and struggled to find words to express how sad and scared I was about whatever was happening to me. I spoke slowly and carefully while fiddling with the flower in my hand and hoped for her comfort and love. We maintained our pace and forward motion, and when I was through, Mom straightened her back and bore her gaze directly ahead.

"Well," she snorted, "I have never been depressed a day in my life, not one day!"

I turned my body toward her as we kept walking, and she continued. "I cannot begin to understand what you are saying. I always have God. I manage all my feelings by praying to God!" She pursed her lips together and smacked her lower lip as she raised her chin, "I wish you could do the same."

I could not. Religion would never be my salvation, nor would it help me shake the inexplicable angst and dread of annihilation I felt in my panic attacks. Nothing could.

There were no words to help me understand what I experienced. Again, no one used the term "panic attack" when I was growing up, not even the doctors we consulted. I didn't understand my biology, my hypersensitive adrenal system that triggered wild physical reactions and blocked all rational thought. The cycle of chronic anxiety caused by feeling alone and disconnected, and the extreme physical overreaction I had to it, repeated again and again, and every attack felt like the one that would kill me. My only defense against the endless attacks was to avoid whatever made me anxious. As a result, I hung on to anything familiar, limiting travel and new experiences.

What if I'd known more about other adoptees' feelings? That it wasn't odd to look in the mirror and wonder who I was and where I came from? Or that it wasn't unusual for us to feel overwhelmed by the subconscious memories of being abandoned at birth or to carry a devastating feeling of rejection with us? What if I had known I wasn't crazy? And that instead, I could learn to manage my losses?

Whenever I told someone how disconnected and alone I felt or how much I wanted to see a person who looked like me, the reaction was always the same: I'd encounter a blank stare and a comment that no one thought about those things, that they weren't important. The response dismissed and diminished me. I wish I'd known I wasn't pathetic, that they simply didn't understand. No one I confided in had been adopted. They were so rooted in place, they never thought twice about it. It wasn't important to them, but it was *everything* to me.

CHAPTER NINE

Self-Preservation

1970

When I was a sophomore in high school, I was surprised and flattered to be asked out by Matt, a senior. I didn't know him well, as he had spent the previous year in England. Our school was small and our families knew each other, so I accepted his invitation to see *Love Story*, the movie of the year. I wore a new outfit for the date, a casual henley-style shirtdress in dusty pink. The evening was okay, not exciting. I didn't spark with him. We didn't share interests or talk about anything personal or profound, but we did continue to date.

A gifted student, Matt achieved a perfect SAT score and was admitted to Dartmouth College, his first choice. We'd been dating for about a year when he went off to college, a departure that left me floundering. I'd spent so much time with him and his senior class friends, I was no longer connected to my peers. I managed by focusing on my academics and painting, and continued the relationship by traveling to Dartmouth for special college weekends, such as home-coming and Winter Carnival.

I loved the Dartmouth campus and felt comfortable with Matt's friends. When he joined a fraternity, I became the chapter's unof-ficial "Little Sister" and enjoyed a protected "hands-off" status. As the "invisible little sister," I was exposed to a much broader group of men than at my homogenous high school. I listened to conversations about women from the brothers' perspectives, both serious and casual, including the occasional crude remark. They talked to one another about sports and competition with bravado and defeat. A few were Olympic athletes. Some brothers were from elite private schools and wealthy families, others from rural public schools and families who struggled. All were successful students, and watching how they han-dled the academic demands at Dartmouth helped me prepare for my own college career. Matt's fraternity brothers demonstrated respect and support, albeit with occasional stupidity and mindlessness. The breadth of their backgrounds was fascinating, introducing me to new worlds. They were a community I felt privileged to be a part of.

I usually drove to New Hampshire with other New Jersey girls whose boyfriends attended Dartmouth. Ride offers were posted on the campus bulletin board, and when I couldn't find one, I took the bus from New York City, but only as a last resort. The bus challenged me as I always suffered a panic attack on that long ride. Still, I wanted to get there more than I wanted to stay home. Home was claustro-phobic, Mom was oppressive, and I'd do almost anything to have a few days of fun with friends. I wanted to feel normal. Each time I took the bus, I'd hope this time would be different, that I would be okay. It wasn't the distance that provoked an attack; I didn't panic when making the trip in a car with someone I knew. Something about being alone with strangers set me off. I worried that a lack of anything familiar would trigger my anxiety and that I couldn't trust anyone to help me. That was the crux of the matter, being alone and not trusting anyone to care. While always seeking the familiar to feel safe, the patterns of being too dependent on my parents and too afraid to take risks persisted. I was a very straitlaced teenager. No one looking at me would've ever guessed I was pushing myself to my limits to achieve something as simple as a weekend away.

I remember standing in the dinge on the lower platform of Port Authority one Friday evening. The fumes and soot turned under yellow lights; the platform was damp and sticky. I looked ridiculous in my tan wool Melton coat with the attached plaid scarf and embossed gold buttons. All the other young people wore denim jackets and had backpacks thrown over their shoulders. Clutching my suitcase, I stepped toward the bus and almost collided with an older woman. She gave me a quick smile, and I seized on that small moment of connection. Maybe I wouldn't feel so alone on this trip.

Outside of the city, we passed old stone houses with gnarly apple orchards and sunlit green meadows. I leaned back and exhaled. The afternoon sun touched my cheek as I watched the scenery slide past—and then it hit.

Abruptly, I stood, as if I could escape what was coming. Embarrassed, I sat back into my seat and noticed the woman who smiled at me sitting across the aisle. My heart was racing and I wondered how bad this attack would be. Would this be the one that finally caused my demise? Stroking my wrist in search of a pulse, I tried to gauge my risk. Then I began to shiver. The woman looked at me, and I knew she saw me shaking. She leaned into the aisle, "Are you ill?"

I was grateful she was concerned but felt as if I were underwater and could only squeak out a meek, "No." She hesitated, turning back to her needlepoint, but glanced at me frequently. My body shuddered as quakes ripped through me. I rubbed back and forth on my forehead, trying to soothe myself. She leaned over again and took my wrist. My pulse was wild, but the warmth of her hand and the pressure of her grasp helped ground me. "Are you sure you're alright?"

My panic was subsiding. The worst was over. I'd survived another one. I was coming back into focus and offered her a small smile and my nodded reply, yes.

The bus came to a stop in the next town, and she gathered her needlepoint, gave me one more glance, and stepped off the bus. I watched young children run to her and wrap themselves around her legs. She looked up and scanned the windows until our eyes met. Holding my gaze, she smiled, and I smiled back. As the bus started to pull away, she hugged the children closer. But she didn't look away from me. She nodded and smiled again.

I turned to look at the road ahead. It was such a wonderful gold, touched with the afternoon sun as it moved through the brown hills.

In the spring of 1972, I was accepted at Skidmore College, which I'd chosen because of its fine arts department. I was also accepted for the summer session at Dartmouth, where I planned to study art history. Matt and I drove to Dartmouth, where I moved into a dorm with three other girls and a stray kitten while Matt lived in his fraternity house. I didn't spend much time with my roommates (or the kitten) because I was usually with Matt and his friends. While my relationship with him remained superficial, it offered me a connection to the Dartmouth community and a familiar world away from home and family. I was using Matt to detach from my family and wasn't proud of it, but it was helping me grow. Since I didn't feel scared or alone there, I could relax and focus on academics. I loved my classes, especially art history, where I aced challenging Blue Book exams and earned the respect of a demanding professor. My success at

Dartmouth surprised me, for, despite being a National Honor Society student, I didn't feel smart. I simply couldn't see myself as valuable or strong. It was imprinted somewhere deep inside me: you are not worthy, you are not important, you are not wanted. Those summer classes uncovered new strengths and interests, and my academic success at Dartmouth raised new possibilities. By the end of the term, I had inched forward in life.

As the summer waned, I was increasingly bored with Matt. Yet I wasn't ready to leave him. In fact, the more I considered breaking up with him, the more my old anxieties resurfaced. I'd replaced one dependance with another—Matt in place of my parents—and the idea of removing Matt threatened to rip open the big black hole at my core once again.

I fantasized about him proposing and how it would frame my life, never mind the fact that I was eighteen and didn't love him. I'd be attached to someone; I'd have less to figure out. Those thoughts were rare, but they did occur, and I was ashamed of them. Despite some burgeoning success at Dartmouth that summer, there was not enough of me yet to appreciate, and new anxieties were looming. I was heading to a new college in the fall. I didn't know anyone there and couldn't imagine what it would be like. Who would I be without Matt and my ties to Dartmouth? Because I needed more time attached to Matt, ending the relationship took another year.

That fall, I headed to Skidmore College in Saratoga Springs, New York, for my freshman year. My major was studio art, and I looked forward to exploring new mediums and being challenged by cutting-edge professors. Most art majors at Skidmore lived on the "Old Campus," and my dorm assignment was Court House, a Victorian-style home complete with a round turret. It was rumored to have a secret underground tunnel that hearkened back to the days of Saratoga residents Lillian Russell and Diamond Jim Brady. I enjoyed my dorm mates, most of us freshman art majors, and we bonded as we walked to the art studios, struggled with assignments, and shared meals. We called ourselves "The Court Street Gang," and I appreciated their friendship and support. Unfortunately, as Skidmore was still primarily a women's college, I depended on Matt, just two hours away, for most of my social life. Traveling to Dartmouth every weekend for fraternity parties didn't cement my Skidmore friendships, and I regret spending so much time with Matt and not strengthening my other relationships.

For sophomore year at Skidmore, my "Court Street Gang" friends and I had different room assignments around campus. With no close friends in my new dorm, I burrowed in and focused on my studies. Second-year classes were significantly more challenging and forced me out of my comfort zone, especially drawing. I'd been a painter in high school, and my only drawing was whimsical and illustrative. Now I struggled with assignments. By comparison, most classmates' drawings were stunning, and I was determined to improve my work. The book *Drawing on the Right Side of the Brain* by Betty Edwards was recommended, and I devoured it, practicing every exercise it suggested. When my drawing professor assigned a self-portrait to the class, I hoped I'd learned enough to do it justice.

Positioning myself in front of the mirror in my dorm room, I pulled a sheet of Bristol toward me. The paper made a soft wafting sound as I placed it on my drawing board. I stared at the empty, white surface and wondered how I'd ever fill it. My new skills were tentative at best, and I knew my only hope was to trust the process suggested in Betty Edwards's book: ignore my conscious mind, disregard labels like "hand" or "nose," and instead focus on the positive and negative space around everything. Supposedly, if I just looked at shapes and followed the outlines without my brain correcting me, I would create an accurate image. Relaxing my mind and softening my eyes, I picked a random starting point and let the graphite glide across the thick paper, the edge of my hand warming as it slid over the soft fibers. Fine black tailings scattered over the page, and my nose twitched with the peppery smell. Focusing on small sections of form, the arc of my shoulder, and the line of my back, I stopped labeling body parts and simply followed the flow of lines around shapes. As I lost myself in work, my room receded, and the sounds of doors slamming and people walking in the busy hallway faded.

Slipping further into a meditative state, I discovered a portrait emerging that surprised me. I had drawn a tri-panel mirror, the kind you might see in a department store dressing room. My reflection was in the center panel of the mirror, but in the other two, I was drawing my mother and Grandma Vincentz. Why would I put them in my *self-portrait*? We didn't look alike; we weren't physically related; we didn't even have shared interests or talents! I stopped working on their images and focused solely on mine. But when I tried to draw myself, my hand was unsure and stumbled around the page. The flow was gone, the pencil dragged and dug into the paper, and my frustration grew. I grabbed my eraser, and before long, only oily rubber crumbs remained where my image had been. I was left feeling itchy, antsy, and exhausted. It was physically uncomfortable to draw myself, and the image I was creating looked like a stranger.

It was easier to draw my mother or, especially, my grandmother. Her face flowed easily from my pencil—but why was she in my self-portrait? I erased and smudged till the paper was ruined and then tried another until I had thrown out a pile of new attempts. It was torture to work on my image. I got up, paced, and ached in every muscle. I didn't want Mom or Grandma in my self-portrait, but I couldn't complete a drawing of myself alone. Eventually, I set the project aside and, for the first time in my life, didn't complete an academic assignment. Convinced the drawing was beyond my technical ability, I didn't want to face the deeper issues of identity that surfaced with this assignment.

As an adoptee, I didn't have anyone who mirrored *me*, who affirmed how I looked and acted. I drew the women who raised me, though I didn't look or act like them. I couldn't form myself unless I was a reflection of others, even in a drawing.

Who am I? There were so many things I hadn't learned about myself—not only the kinds of things any young person has yet to understand but also behaviors I'd never seen reflected, instincts I hadn't observed in my adoptive parents, things programmed by nature, not nurture.

The feelings of being dropped from the sky, of profound loneliness and emptiness, were always with me no matter how hard I tried to ignore them. I was nineteen years old and still didn't have a sense of self, a solid core. The drawing I couldn't complete slapped me in the face with the fact that the big black hole in my center was still there.

I'd spent a second summer at Dartmouth between my freshman and sophomore years, not as a student this time working a summer job and being at Dartmouth with Matt and his friends.

After renting a room just down the hill from Matt's fraternity, I worked at the local supermarket, assigned to the delicatessen department. As a lifelong vegetarian, I couldn't have been placed in a less suitable role. I gagged every time I had to stab a chicken onto the rotisserie or asked customers to point to whatever meat they wanted. I saw Matt daily, but our relationship was just a bad habit by then. We hung out at his fraternity, where an ever-present cache of friends kept us distracted and amused, and we rarely spent time alone together. Matt was heading into his senior year. I knew he was nervous about life after college; he was edgy and often in a bad mood, so our time together wasn't fun.

Matt had a single room tucked into the eaves of his stately Greek-Revival fraternity house. The room was tight with Matt's bed against the wall, open shelves piled high with books, and a small refrigerator next to his desk, its thick black extension cord snaking through the room. One hot summer day I sat cross-legged on the bed, trying to think of something to do, while Matt stood at his desk. The room was deathly quiet and still, and the small space held the stench of dirty hockey jerseys. When the smell became unbearable, I got up to get some fresh air.

Suddenly, inexplicably, Matt snapped—completely out of the blue. He was enraged and, in his anger, he slapped me, then pushed me violently, sending me flying across the room. I stumbled, hit my shoulder, and fell, my face pressed against the side of his gunmetal desk. I struggled to get up and gulped dust as I toppled a chair, twisting my body to stand gape-mouthed as Matt continued pacing and yelling, his hands gesturing high and low. I'd known him for three years and nothing like this had ever happened. It was entirely without context. To this day, I have no idea why or remember what could have possibly led up to it. I don't remember our conversation or a disagreement of any kind.

After a few frozen moments, I turned and walked out of the room. I didn't ask him what was happening or confront him. I just left. Some self-protective instinct told me to go. I hyperfocused on the grimy red carpet and the smell of stale beer as I floated down the stairs. The sound of the television fired from the "tube room," and I wondered who was in there but immediately realized that whoever it was, they were no longer my friend. I was leaving Matt and everything connected to him. Reaching the front door, I stepped outside and headed toward my rented room in a daze.

The breeze was warm and sunlight dappled through bright green leaves and scattered across the blue Connecticut River. An hour earlier, the perfect summer day would have thrilled me. Now, it felt as strange as all things feel in the wake of sudden loss. I threw my clothes into a suitcase and got on the next bus to New York City. I didn't tell Matt I was leaving. I didn't ask anyone for help. I called my parents to tell them I was coming home, and Mom was stunned. It was the middle of the summer. What about my job? I don't remember what I told her, but it wasn't the truth.

At that point I had no idea Matt's family had a history of trauma and physical abuse, nor did I know anything about domestic violence. No one talked about it in those days, and I certainly had never seen anything like that in my own home. I don't know why I walked out. It was gut instinct. Something in my DNA gave me the fortitude to leave. There was no hesitation, no self-doubt, no debate. It was such unexpected behavior for me. Instead of shrinking in the moment, I stood firm, acted in my own best interest, and got out. At the time I didn't understand it as instinct or built-in strength, nor did I suddenly morph into a brave and independent woman. My anxieties remained, but this was the first glimpse of there being more to me than I understood, a spark I would recognize many years later.

I never spoke with Matt again. There was no final conversation or official breakup. At one point, his mother called my mother and asked if I would see him again. When I refused, my mother pressed me but ultimately accepted my answer, a definitive "*No!*" I never told her the truth, though I don't know why. He shoved me with such sudden, inexplicable rage there was no question in my mind I would never see him again. There was something explosive in that man, and I wanted no part of it. After three years, I didn't grieve the relationship; I only felt relief.

Many years later, Matt's sister called me. Though we didn't know each other well, I accepted her invitation to lunch. Throughout the meal, she talked about her brother in the most glowing terms. It was odd. I was married now, and he was married. Why was she conversing about him? She wanted me to agree that he was wonderful and successful, which was bizarre and uncomfortable. I finally put my fork down and looked her in the eye. "Your brother once threw me across a room; I don't hold fond memories of him."

Tears filled her eyes, and she bowed her head. "I wondered if anything like that ever happened to you." She paused and looked up. "I think Matt is violent in his marriage as well."

Then she told me about their father's bipolar depression and abuse and their mother's alcoholism. Once a brilliant Harvard graduate, their father suffered a mental breakdown and became violent, most often with Matt. The high school year Matt spent in England had been arranged to get him away from their father and protect him.

As I listened to her shocking stories, two memories flooded in. One was of an afternoon at Matt's house when we were in high school. We were upstairs when I heard a yelp, and Matt's youngest sister came tearing through the hall in a panic, ran into her bedroom, and slammed the door with a shriek. A moment later, their father roared up the stairs with a force of fury I'd never seen before. He ran at her door, yelling, his arm raised. Matt grabbed me and hustled me out of the house as quickly as he could, driving me home without acknowledging what had just happened, and I didn't want to embarrass him by asking. The rage I'd witnessed was terrifying, but I put it out of my mind as "none of my business."

The other memory was a weekend drive to New Hampshire with Matt's mother and sister, who offered to drop me off at Dartmouth on their way to visit friends. Four liter-sized Diet Pepsi bottles were rolling around on the back floor of the car, used bottles, I noted, and his sister cautioned me not to drink from them as they were "Mom's special soda." Now and then, their mother would ask for a bottle and take generous slugs as she drove along. I had no idea the "special soda" was spiked with alcohol. It never occurred to me that my boyfriend's mother, driving me from New Jersey to New Hampshire, was drinking for the entire six-hour drive.

As Matt's sister talked that day at lunch, I was shocked to think I'd never been aware of these things and marveled at the ability of a family to hide such trauma from the world. While I was sorry to hear about all they'd endured, I was grateful I'd escaped. Thank God Matt had cracked enough to forewarn me about a continued relationship with him, and thank God I'd been born with the strength to get out.

CHAPTER TEN

Finding My Voice

1974–1975

I transferred to Colgate University at the start of my junior year to pursue a literature major, having completed my fine arts major at Skidmore. I'd experienced Colgate through a monthlong exchange program the previous year and fallen in love with the bucolic campus: the storied Willow Walk, its trees weeping to the water below; a soft, blue stream curling under its arched bridge; broad, green fields; handsome stone buildings trimmed in white; and the Chenango Valley all around, rising and falling like the English countryside. From my first days at Colgate, I'd felt a sense of place, of deep belonging. It was where I was supposed to be. I was thrilled to arrive as a Colgate student in the fall of 1974.

One evening, the week before classes began, I decided to walk "downtown," as we called the small rural village of Hamilton. Particular bars in the village were favorites of Colgate students, and my first stop was The Hub, always the most crowded. When I opened the door, I was blasted by the heat and noise of the crowd, and the smell of spilled beer and wet wood crept over me as my shoes sucked to the floor. Hormones hovered above the crowd, thick and expectant, and the clamor of hundreds of eager conversations was deafening. As I pushed through, pink, sweaty faces flashed in and out of view, and amber beer bottles glistened as arms raised to allow me to pass. Light spread through hovering smoke, and beer saturated every molecule of air. Every breath tasted of it.

I was glad to see a girl from my dorm who introduced me to a group of her friends. Their table was crammed with pitchers of beer, and I gladly accepted a glass, though within minutes, a new wave of students pushed into the room, and I lost sight of my friend. Looking around awkwardly, I considered leaving, but one of the guys standing near me turned with a smile and said hello. His name was Greg and he was on the hockey team at Colgate. Every now and then as we talked, he stepped up to the pool table to take his turn, and I watched the game with partial interest while I finished my beer. The air grew thick as the crowd swelled further and I was jostled and squished. I wanted to leave but decided to stick it out a little longer. Having just arrived on campus, I wanted to meet new people, and here I was, out on my own doing that. Things would be okay at Colgate. I could handle this move! There was something exciting about it, daring, even.

Greg kept pouring me cold beer, filling my glass whenever it hit the halfway point, and I kept drinking. It was refreshing and gave me something to do when the conversation lulled. At one point, instead of pouring me a glass, he lifted the pitcher to my lips and instructed me to drink up. Why I obeyed is a mystery, but I lifted my chin and chugged a throatful of cold ale. I heard chants and cheers and was embarrassed—what was I doing? This wasn't at all like me! Before I could gather my wits, the world blurred, and a faceless sea of black and brown shadows swirled around me. I grabbed the side of the pool table to steady myself. Greg put down his pool cue and asked me if I wanted a ride home, and I was grateful for his offer.

I was surprised he had a "muscle car," black with a bold yellow racing stripe. I'd never gone out with the kind of guy who drove a car designed to telegraph machismo, but I pushed a flash of concern aside and got in.

Streetlights flashed overhead, my forehead fell against the cold window, and the next thing I knew, he was guiding me into a place that was not my dorm. I had no idea where I was and could barely walk, but Greg was behind me, holding my waist and shoulder as he pushed me into a place so bright it startled me. There was motion to my right, where two or three people were playing cards. They nodded as Greg greeted them and then pressed me into his bedroom. It was pitch black there and I lost all sense of direction. When I tried to speak, I couldn't form words. He thrust me onto his bed and climbed on top of me, kissing and groping me as I drifted in and out of consciousness.

I tried to push him off but had no strength. He came at me like a viper, his breath hot and sour. I turned my head away, and the room spun. He climbed all over me, but I couldn't lift my arms to stop him. Weak and fading, all I wanted to do was sleep. The sweet scent of a warm bed swirled through my brain, and my head sank into the pillow. My eyes closed as I let go, melting into his mattress. I didn't care what happened. I just wanted to sleep. Succumbing, I felt myself falling, falling—until, from somewhere far below, I heard a voice shout, "NO!"

My eyes flashed open, and I heard it again, "NO!" This time it was deep and resonant, and I felt it in the back of my brain. Something was telling me, *No, this would not happen to me. This would not be a part of my life story.* I summoned every ounce of strength and shoved him with so much rage and disgust that he fell to the floor with one defiant push.

Peeling tangled sheets from my legs, I staggered toward the sound in the living room, where his roommates were playing cards.

They looked up at me, cigar smoke circling, scotch glistening on the rocks in glasses. Then one of them nodded my way, saying, "That was quick!" and they all snickered. Someone slapped a card down, and they turned back to their game. I lurched for the door and ran out into the freezing, pitch-black night.

The cold air hit my face. I tried to get my bearings but had no idea where I was. I didn't know how I got there. I didn't know where the campus was. It was dark as far as I could see, and I turned in circles, searching for any spark of light. Far away, a small star hovered alone in the sky—but it wasn't a star. It was the gold dome of the Colgate chapel, the pinnacle of campus. Shivering, groggy, I started toward that gold spark. It was so far away, I didn't know how I'd make it there. All I could do was start down the nearby road and hope it led me closer.

I passed the empty football stadium. Dark bleachers loomed against the sky, and the tang of cold metal stuck in my throat. Thick woods stretched along a dank, rotting streambed and I recoiled before hurrying past. My skin was stiff with cold. My feet were numb. A mantra looped through my brain—"Just get home, just get home, just get home"—and I obeyed the command like a soldier. I was trying to save myself. Traumatized and alone, I kept walking toward that dome in the sky. I was focused and determined. Even as I was doing it, it surprised me.

I found myself on the main road leading to campus, but there was no traffic on the street, nor a soul stirring around 3:00 a.m. Slowly, signs of civilization came into view: a streetlight and a couple of houses. Though a long walk was still ahead, I knew I was getting closer.

Finally, I glimpsed a familiar brick facade and my heart quickened. Racing to the door, fumbling with my key, I stumbled inside, went limp, slid against the wall, fell to the floor, and passed out. I don't know how long I slumped against the wall, unconscious, but when I came to, I climbed upstairs and into bed. My desk lamp glowed warm, and golden brown shadows gathered around my room. The dorm was quiet and still, and I pictured everyone safely inside the strong brick walls. Pulling my blankets into thick waves around my shoulders, I closed my eyes and surrendered to a deep, dreamless sleep.

Of the few people I shared my assault story with, no one suggested I do anything about it. Most friends looked shocked or uncomfortable and, more than anything, seemed surprised that Greg had chosen me as a conquest. It's shocking to think back on their responses now, in light of the awareness and empowerment we have today.

In 2017, when the MeToo Movement dominated the headlines, I googled Greg. He had become a politician and served on his town council. I wondered about all the people he might have mistreated and what dark secrets he kept. We were twenty years old when he plied me with alcohol and tried to rape me. I wondered about his wife and if he had a daughter. For a few minutes, I imagined punching him in the face, pulling my arm back and letting my fist slam into his nose with force, knocking him down and seeing the dark red blood running down his chin. I imagined him looking small and stunned as I walked away.

Yet whenever I thought of that night, it wasn't Greg who came to mind first. It was always me and how I managed to get away safely. Because I had always seen myself as weak and easily overwhelmed, moments of uncharacteristic strength, like this one and when I walked out on Matt, confused me. It was difficult for me to overcome my low self-worth or recognize competence in myself. Certainly I never would have imagined that courage was built into my DNA.

With Greg, I thought I was lucky to have escaped a bad situation, and like many victims of sexual assault, I blamed myself for drinking too much (it never occurred to me I might also have been drugged) and for accepting a ride home from someone I'd just met. But now I look back and know it wasn't luck. I was born with tools and traits that got me out of that situation: fortitude, determination, physical strength, and anger. But I would need much more knowledge about who I was and where I came from before I could see any of that.

That fall, the trauma of the assault further eroded my self-worth. While I'd made strides—ending my dependence on my parents, walking away from Matt, and buoyed by academic success—they weren't enough. In fact, I felt emptier than ever. I was at a new school, starting a new major, and had no relationship. Everything that previously defined me was gone, even before that traumatic first week. I was a mess as I transferred into Colgate and I soon psychologically "hit a wall." I had to figure out why I was so detached from my own life. I knew it was time to deal with that big black hole at my core, no matter how humiliating and painful the exploration might be.

The problem was I didn't know what caused that void. Lacking information about common adoptee experiences or a path directing me to the source of my pain, I had no discernable way to deal with it. Something was wrong with me, but what?

I remember wishing everyone at Colgate knew and liked me, yet wishing I was popular made me feel superficial and pathetic. If I'd known it was common for adoptees to feel unwanted, to long for approval and acceptance, maybe I could have better understood my embarrassing desire. Sadly, I also felt helpless to create change in my life. The feelings of helplessness and hopelessness were two more adoption consequences I hadn't known about.

Detached and passive, I didn't do anything to integrate into the campus community. I envied students strolling along the Willow

Path or throwing Frisbees on the lawn. I didn't know how to become one of them. I was a body going through the motions of everyday life. I was empty. If it was my job to find or create my solid core, I didn't know how.

In her brilliant book *The Primal Wound: Understanding the Adopted Child*, Nancy Newton Verrier explains that when adoptees are deprived of knowledge or a context for their preconscious sense of loss, they often feel "abnormal, sick, or crazy for having those feelings" and are often left confused by their own behavior. She writes, "What the child has missed is the security and serenity of oneness with the person who gave birth to him, a continuum of bonding from prenatal to postnatal life. This is the profound connection for which the adoptee forever yearns. It is this yearning which leaves him often feeling hopeless, helpless, empty, and alone. . . . That period immediately after birth, when the infant has made the transition from the . . . security of the womb to the cold, bright, alien world of postnatal life, is a crucial period. It is a time when a baby needs to be in proximity to his mother in order to find the world safe and welcoming. . . . At that time the mother is the whole world for the baby, and his connection to her is essential to his sense of well-being and wholeness. . . . abandonment is a kind of death, not only of the mother but of part of the Self, that core-being or essence of oneself which makes one feel whole."

The Primal Wound was written in 1991, so I didn't have the benefit of its affirming knowledge in 1974. When I fell apart that fall, I was oblivious to all that lay beneath my unraveling.

Instinct guided me to hunker down, and I disappeared into books and poetry, listened to a lot of music, wrote in my journals, and kept to myself. The lyrics of "Your Bright Baby Blues," a favorite Jackson Browne song, haunted me:

> *You watch yourself from the sidelines*
> *Like your life is a game you don't mind playing*
> *To keep yourself amused*

Why was I watching myself from the sidelines? Why was I so confused about my own life? I'd been so busy trying to be the perfect adoptee and protect myself from further rejection, I never figured out who I genuinely was. Now I saw how empty and lost that had left me. I was like a baby lying on its back, flailing its arms in the air, incapable of lifting itself up. I was infantile. I did not have a "sense of well-being and wholeness" or a "core-being," and I couldn't figure out how to create one.

It is embarrassing to say these things now, but they are as accurate and honest as I can be. It is a painful time to remember.

While I felt helpless, there was still plenty I found joy in. I loved the campus, and every season held incredible beauty. Moments that took my breath away graced every day. In the late spring, climbing the hill to classes, sunlight would poke through the thick canopy of leaves, shooting a thousand colors of green and strobing beams of gold in and out. From the top of campus, the Chenango Valley spread in every direction, hills bending gently toward the horizon, an immense sky resting over them as peaceably as firelight on a sleeping cat's back. The autumn foliage was glorious, flaming colors glowing from within, crisp blue skies above. Snow came early and stayed late. By the end of October, the stars seemed to freeze against the sky and turn to snow, falling to dust the hills whose winter blues and browns created a cozy patchwork. One January, it snowed every day of the month, and late March still held melting drifts, small grime-speckled ones like Robert Frost described as "blown-away papers the rain had brought to rest." I loved it all and never considered leaving, even when I felt lost and barely there. I was where I needed to be. This was a good place to rest while trying to figure out the sorrow and emptiness inside of me.

As the spring semester of 1975 arrived, I emerged, some survival instinct pushing me to reach out and make connections. My roommate Sarah and her boyfriend founded the Colgate Student Theater and were preparing an original musical production. I agreed to help choreograph and teach a tap dancing number for the show, though I'd never had a professional tap dancing lesson. My only experience had been on a dance team in high school, but Sarah assured me I could do it. I trusted her and was forever grateful she encouraged me. The Colgate Student Theater was inclusive, regardless of experience, and I discovered a much-needed community in that theater troupe, their camaraderie soothing me like water down a parched throat.

At our first tap dance rehearsal, I hoped my limited knowledge wouldn't be glaring, and starting with basic steps, we learned and laughed together. I noticed one actor with a laid-back vibe, a twinkle in his eye, and an intriguing smile, who turned out to have a true gift with words. He could toss out lines that veered from clever puns to brilliant poetry. Before the show's last performance, Lonny and I were dating and would develop one of the most genuine connections I'd ever experienced. I felt safe in that relationship, free to be vulnerable and authentic. The ten pounds I'd put on the previous semester didn't seem to matter, and I felt seen, loved, and beautiful. Even visiting his family was terrific. His parents were open and casual in ways mine were not, and I loved the delicious made-from-scratch pasta they prepared on Sundays. There was laughter around their dinner table, and everything about his family was comfortable for me.

Though Lonny and I dated for two years, the relationship wasn't without challenges. I wanted commitment, but he didn't. I kept hanging on (though unlike with Matt, I stayed in this relationship because I was in love) and I was can't-eat-can't-sleep devastated when he broke up with me. I didn't recognize how much the loss of this relationship echoed the losses I'd experienced as an adoptee—someone I truly loved left me. I wasn't worth their commitment, and I would never be a part of their wider family. The layers of loss were heavy, and I didn't understand them as I tried to heal my deeply broken heart. Separation is always a charged issue for an adoptee, and while the pain of loss isn't erased by awareness of deeper issues, that clarity is necessary to process and fully move past any of life's losses.

But the spring when Lonny and I first met was happy. I was falling head over heels for him, the play rehearsals were great fun, and my classes were terrific. One of my classes touched on childhood development, and the research was fascinating, especially early childhood development. The exquisite awareness of infants, at and even before birth, the concept of preconscious and preverbal thought, and somatic memories—everything I read lit up my brain. I recognized the truth of my own life in this research and realized I had those experiences and held such memories. Maybe this research could lead me to understand the emptiness at my center.

Delving deeper, I discovered a universe of work on identity and adoption and read books, articles, and anything I could get my hands on, seeing myself in all of it.

It was a relief to learn I wasn't alone. The big black hole inside was a universal experience for adoptees, as was the drive to search and reconnect with one's birth mother. There were many countries, even states within the US, where adoption records were open, and one statistic said 96 percent of birth mothers wished to meet the child they surrendered, even if the child was the result of rape. My reading also educated me on international and interracial adoption, and the complex challenges they presented. I couldn't imagine the disconnect those adoptees felt and all they lost despite gaining a family.

Now, as a young adult bolstered with concrete knowledge, I considered initiating a search for my birth mother, but I still wasn't ready. (Never mind that there was no internet or sites for DNA testing, genealogy, and ancestry tracing like there are today, and I didn't have one speck of information with which to start a search.) This undertaking also felt like a betrayal of my adoptive parents and a huge risk. I already had a demanding mother. What if my birth mother was also? It would be too much to bear. Still, I desperately wanted to see someone who looked like me and discover where I came from. The ideal situation, I decided, would be a fly-on-the-wall scenario—one where I could watch my birth mother without having to reveal myself or get involved with her.

Meanwhile, I was serious about further research and petitioned the university to create an independent study on identity and adoption. When my final paper received an A+, I felt validated and was inspired to send a copy of it to my adoption agency, along with some basic questions about my biological parents. I wasn't sure the agency would share anything about my origins with me, so the commendation of my paper felt necessary. It was my credential into their world, into the study and practice of adoption, rather than my world, the *experience* of it—one completely different from the other. With my Colgate-approved paper, I was saying, *It's not just me. I'm not crazy, I'm not a rebellious (read: bad) adoptee.* I was sending external validation in order to ask an agency about my life because otherwise my needs and rights were not recognized or respected. I was trying to say, "*Research* says this and *all adoptees* feel this, so it's only natural I should ask. Please don't shut me down. Please help me find the answers I need." I was finally finding my voice.

CHAPTER ELEVEN

A Red-Letter Day

1977

In May 1977, I walked across the Colgate commencement stage, grateful to have had the opportunity to pursue my passion for art and literature but aware my education didn't leave me very employable. Fortunately, Mom and Dad believed in education and were happy not only for my Colgate BA but encouraged me to pursue graduate studies at Cornell University.

During my Colgate commencement weekend, a friend's brother asked me if I needed a place to stay at Cornell. He was a student there and explained that his fraternity rented rooms to women in the summer months, and there was still availability.

"Oh God no," I exclaimed, "I don't want to spend my summer with a bunch of fraternity men!"

He laughed and shrugged his shoulders. "Okay, but here's the name of the guy you should ask for if you change your mind."

It seemed like the last thing I needed. Cornell had given me a summer job with housing in the graduate dorm, but I stuffed the slip of paper into my pocket anyway.

When I arrived in Ithaca, I was disappointed to find the graduate dorm was a depressing gray high-rise, so I reached for the scrap of paper I'd kept. It turned out the fraternity house on Edgemoor Lane was a Tudor mansion towering over a deep green gorge, and the sound of rushing water played in the background. Suddenly, living with some fraternity men for the summer didn't seem like such a bad idea.

Checking the paper for the contact name, I pulled open the heavy wood doors and walked into the dark foyer of Chi Phi. Ahead of me, windows looked onto the tops of trees descending into the gorge. They were lush and alive with a million strokes of green flashing and sunlight chasing layer on layer of shadows. A cool breeze scuttered across the room and brushed past me; goosebumps raised on my legs. I immediately knew I wanted to stay there. I heard voices and followed them into the paneled library where two fraternity brothers sat near a massive fireplace and a large leaded glass window. They looked up as I entered.

"Hi. I'm looking for Brian Murdock?"

One of the brothers looked at me. He was cute, with blond surfer hair, a chiseled face, and a bright smile.

"I'm Brian."

I explained how their friend Bobby told me I could rent a room for the summer and was interested in doing so. The brother looked uncomfortable. "I'm not Brian," he admitted sheepishly and pointed through another door. "I think he's downstairs."

His friend laughed, and I was both embarrassed and annoyed. For a moment, I weighed the behavior of fraternity men against the house's beauty, situated as if in the treetops, the mesmerizing sound of water tumbling below, and decided yes, it was worth it.

The brother claiming to be Brian turned out to be Rick, who later told me they'd been glued to the window as I arrived, and he thought I was cute and liked my smile. My first impression of him was his handsome face, blond hair, and the way he made my heart flutter.

A few days later, a casual comment piqued our interest in each other. We'd been talking about places we'd lived or visited, places we enjoyed. I said I could never live in the middle of the country because it was too far from an ocean, and Rick replied he felt the same way but had never heard anyone else say that. He invited me to watch the Fourth of July fireworks on the Cornell quad, where our conversation flowed, and neither of us could stop smiling. The fireworks that night were big and bold, which I usually found gut-rattling and scary, but as these exploded, blossoming against the sky with electric color and cascading stars, I felt happy and safe.

Rick and I grew closer in the following weeks, staying up most of the night talking, the streetlights glowing through my window. We discovered how much we shared, and it felt safe to be open and honest about myself. Rick was shyly romantic. He admitted to writing a poem about me but never had the nerve to show it to me. One night he froze a rose in a cup of water, and we watched as the ice slowly melted around the suspended bloom. Rick made fruit salads for dinner and thoroughly cleaned up before he sat down to enjoy his meal. I don't know why that impressed me, but cleaning up reflected good manners in a kitchen used by a house full of people, and, as a vegetarian, I appreciated someone eating fruit salad for dinner! I decided he must come from a proper family that taught him well.

It surprised me to feel such a deep connection with Rick. He was working on his MBA, and though I stereotyped business majors as shallow, there was much about him I warmed to. He was kind, considerate, and intelligent, and I sensed something below the surface that was quiet but powerful. Rick was unlike anyone I'd known before, and I fell in love quickly, even though I knew very little about

him outside of the basic facts: he was an accomplished distance runner, loved the outdoors, admired the arts, and had been president
of the fraternity. He told me he'd moved every two years during
childhood, and his family lived out West. Otherwise, I didn't know
anything about them, though I didn't judge anyone based on their
family. Given my experience, family members were entirely independent entities.

As I settled into a new routine at Cornell, I forgot about the letter
I'd sent to my adoption agency a month earlier, the letter with a copy
of my A+ research paper and questions I hoped they would answer:
What was my ethnic identity? Was there any available medical infor-
mation? Did either parent suffer from anxiety? Why was I given away?
What did they look like? Where were they from?

I'd put the letter out of my mind because I was prepared for disappointment. Adoption law protects secrecy above all else, especially
in New Jersey, and I had no idea if the agency would respond. But
when I least expected it, an envelope from the agency was tossed
into the mail pile in Chi Phi's foyer. There were two pages, typed on
translucent onion skin with whatever "nonidentifying information"
they could share. Shaking, I took the envelope outside to the bright
June sun.

I was twenty-two years old, reading a description of my birth
mother and father for the first time in my life. Holding the thin papers
above emerald grass and gray pavement, the type lay on pale paper, a
visual whisper instead of the shout I expected, and I read them and
reread them and reread them again.

My nineteen-year-old mother was five feet four inches tall, had
blue eyes, blonde curly hair, fair skin, and was "Protestant, of English-
Irish descent." My nineteen-year-old father was five feet eleven inches
tall with "a large build, dark brown hair, brown eyes, a medium complexion" and was of "Irish descent, Catholic in religion." They broke
up before my birth mother knew she was pregnant, and he didn't

know I existed. She "felt there was no basis for an ongoing relationship and was looking forward to marriage to a young man then in
the Navy."

My mother was "a twirler in high school and was active, outgoing,
and popular. She was voted 'Miss High School' in her senior year, an
award based on scholarship, school activities, and beauty. She sang in
the high school chorus." She had "an interesting and happy personality
and a sense of humor." My father was "attending college and planning
to be a teacher of English and History." His mother was a school-
teacher. His father was a fire coordinator for the local fire department.

The agency wrote, "The record describes [my mother] as intelligent, stable, and quite mature for her age. She seemed to have made
her decision for adoption based on what she felt would be best, and
she consistently followed through on her plan without allowing herself to be swayed by her emotions."

I read those two pages so many times I felt like I'd sucked the
words off the pages and fit them as deeply inside of myself as I could.
I didn't want to forget one fact or confuse anything in case it was
all I'd ever know. It was so little, really, but for the first time in my
life, I could imagine real people and an actual lineage. The image of
the fifteen-year-old streetwalker evaporated. I'd inherited blue eyes
from my mother and brown hair from my father. I was Irish-English.
The descriptions helped. They gave me a backstory, but now I wanted
more. I wanted to see these people, see myself in them. I couldn't
picture the strangers described in the letter or feel a connection with
them. I was looking at words but wanted to see my mother's face.

The letter said my birth parents were from a "distant state," and
I tried to guess which one—would it be somewhere with a large Irish
population? Massachusetts (thinking Boston) or Illinois (maybe
Chicago)? The letter said my father was studying to teach history or
English, and I wondered where he taught. My mother was portrayed
as a mature and caring young woman, someone I was sure would want

to meet me. My placement seemed lovely, the perfect adoption scenario, an attractive and thoughtful birth mother and healthy families.

As it turned out, the information I received many years later, both in person and when I read my actual file, was very different. My birth parents were not from a distant state but from a town in New York, an hour and a half from where I grew up in New Jersey. My birth father was a retired state trooper, not a professor, and had blue eyes, not brown. And my mother? Well, the agency had very different notes about her too.

The letter I received in the summer of 1977 defended the myth of a perfect adoption. There was a self-congratulatory tone as if to say, "We took care of everything. You should be happy where you are and with what you know. You don't need anything more."

The letter reminded me, the adoptee, I only had a right to the information they chose to tell me. I shouldn't worry about more profound questions of identity or yearn to find the family I was biologically and historically connected to. I didn't need to know the mother I was physiologically bonded with for nine months. The agency believed a baby could be given to strangers, and their love and care were all it needed to thrive.

The laws that mandated the protection of adoption secrets were created in a culture of shame. The shame of both the birth and adoptive parents preempted the rights of the adoptee to know their heritage and family of origin—knowledge necessary to fully actualize themselves. The baby was seen as an empty vessel into which the adoptive parents would pour their love and caring, making the child happy, the parents proud, and the birth mother and father (if he was aware) absolved.

But that's not how it really works. Birth mothers don't simply forget the experience of carrying, bearing, and blindly relinquishing a child. Adoptive parents can't ignore their infertility and genetic demise. And babies aren't blank slates. They are complex human beings for whom separation from their biological mother is an indelible and devastating experience. Maintaining the secrets of adoption isn't in the best interest of anyone in the "adoption triangle"; they primarily dismiss and harm the *individual* traded between families through no fault, or choice, of their own. The adoptee is, after all, a unique, independent individual—not forever a baby. They grow up and become adults who realize their rights were taken from them when they could not defend themselves.

Shortly after receiving the letter from the adoption agency, I read about a national database to reunite adoptees and birth parents. Given the description of my birth mother in the agency's letter, my curiosity and courage were unleashed, and I decided to take the next steps to find her. I immediately sent my information to the database, believing there was a good chance we'd be reunited. She sounded lovely and caring, and I was sure she'd also be looking for me.

But as months, then years, went by with no response, it dawned on me that she wasn't searching, and the idea of continued rejection by my birth mother shocked me. The agency described a mature and caring woman. I couldn't imagine she didn't want to find me.

Find me.

Those were powerful words, and in my disappointment I realized *I wanted to be found*, which was very different from me wanting to find her. To be found, someone has to be looking for you, someone has to want you. All my life I engaged in the magical thinking that *I would be found*. Now I had to process the fact that she might not want to find me or want to be found by me. That was too painful to accept, so I told myself she simply didn't know about the database. And if that was true, there seemed no chance we'd ever meet. There weren't any other avenues available at the time—no DNA sites and no social media.

What were my chances of finding her without any identifying information needed to start a traditional search? I desperately wanted to know where I came from and see someone who looked like me, spoke like me, had mannerisms like me, and maybe even laughed like me. And that drive would never leave me, even as any hope of searching stalled. Years went by where I felt as if I were standing in front of an immense vault, a tower of black steel thick with rivets, bolts, and dials, and nothing but hope to break into it. Pushing my desire aside, I told myself I'd try again in the future.

CHAPTER TWELVE

To Have and to Hold

1977–1979

R ick and I fell in love during the summer of '77, and in May
1978, Rick completed his MBA and accepted a job in California. There was no question I would go with him, though the idea of
moving across the country was terrifying. I was committed to Rick,
so I decided to be brave and take the risk. Leaving everything familiar
stirred up my anxieties, but I had been managing my usual apprehen-
sions well, keeping levels just below the panic threshold, and assumed
I could continue to keep attacks at bay.

We spent a month meandering across the States before he started
his new job, and while that was fun, there were places along the
way—wild, wide-open spaces—that unnerved me and made me feel
vulnerable and alone, even with Rick by my side. At points during our
cross-country expedition, I was desperate to manage my fear and told
myself some pretty crazy things to help me get through. Not long after
we settled in Los Angeles, I took a writing class and wrote about the
trip and the bizarre thoughts I'd entertained to get by. Embarrassed

by my juvenile behavior, I wrote as if those thoughts were the musings of an anxious character in my story. When I read the story to the class, another student commented, "Wow! How did you make all that up?" I was too ashamed to admit those were actually *my* thoughts.

Here are excerpts from the story, which was written in diary format:

June 17

We're heading West, me and this guy I think will marry me. We've been on the road about five hours now, and I don't know this territory very well, though I've heard the names of some of the towns. The roads are winding. Once in a while we pass a car going in the other direction, and it's usually an older couple riding along, all dressed up. They always seem to know where they are going, their noses are straight ahead, and they aren't looking at the scenery as if it's new to them. Here I sit with this guy who I sure hope loves me the way he says he does.

. . . I think Buffalo is just a couple of hours north of here, maybe less, and Buffalo has a big airport. They probably have lots of flights to Newark. I mean, if I really wanted to, if I really had to, I could get Clint to drive me to Buffalo, and in a few hours, I could be home. I could telephone my parents, and they would meet me in Newark. Or I could even call them from the next filling station we pass, and maybe by the time we get to Buffalo, they could have gotten on a plane to meet us there in Buffalo to take me home. You know you can always get home nowadays. There are airports all over the place.

June 21

We're getting pretty far West now. I don't even know anyone who lives west of the Mississippi. But that's O.K. It doesn't matter. Clint loves me. Things are going really well. We're going to be our own family now. If I had to, though, I wonder how fast I could get back to New Jersey from here? I mean, if a person were feeling kinda strange being so far from everything that they knew, they might want to be able to get home. Fast. Well, first I'd have to get to the airport. The map we have is a very good one, it has little airplanes next to all the towns that have airports out here. Drawings of little planes for little airports, and of jet planes for big airports. I like to keep track of the towns with airports. I notice some of them as we drive through, and they aren't really airports. They are strips where little planes can take off, and there are a lot of small planes parked around that are probably owned by rich ranchers. But I could get some guy to fly me to the nearest big airport, and I could get a flight from there back to New Jersey. First, I would have to find the guy in the overalls who always hangs out at the airport fixing planes and looking after things, and I would have to ask him who would be willing to fly me to the next biggest airport. Then he would wipe off his hands and scratch his head and think of someone who wasn't busy, and then he'd go over to his office and call them up and explain the story, and then they would have to drive out from their ranch and get the plane all ready and everything before we could take off. That's a long time, but they'd all be nice and do their best, feeling really good doing such a nice thing for someone who needed help.

June 22

What if the guy with the overalls at the little airport wouldn't help me? What if he just didn't care that I had to get home? What if he didn't understand and let me cry and everything? What would happen to me? I've been looking at the map, and there's usually a little airport every one-hundred-fifty miles or so. If the guy at one airport was mean like that, Clint and I could jump back in the car and speed on down to the next airport. I wonder how fast this old Pinto can drive? I mean, if we really had to drive fast? I mean, if I were about to lose my mind, I was so scared. But what if the Highway Patrol stopped the car you were speeding in? You would have to take the time to explain that you had to get to this other airport 150 miles away, and this guy would probably never believe the reason. After all, I'd be sitting there plain as day, and it certainly wouldn't seem to him like everything was disintegrating.

June 23

We sure are out in the middle of nowhere now. We can drive a hundred miles without seeing a town, then, the town could be only a filling station and a grocery store. I don't see any more airplanes on the map. I wonder how people survive out here. What if something happened to them? Where is the nearest hospital? There's probably some old lady out on a ranch fifty miles from here who has had some doctoring experience and who they'd take you to if you drove a spike through your foot or something, but I mean, what if you had to get to a hospital? Somewhere where they have special gasses and things. I mean, what if you were losing your mind and you had to get somewhere where they could knock you out and save you? At a hospital, they could knock a person out with some of that gas they use for operations and put them on a plane, and by the time they woke up, they would be wherever they had to be, and they would be alright. But just some old lady on a farm who knows something about delivering babies and setting cow's legs wouldn't be able to help someone like that.

I wonder if someone loved you and you asked them to knock you out, I mean really hit you and knock you out, like in the movies, if they would do that, I mean if it meant it would save your life or something?

June 24

You know, probably a person who loved you would feel very strange if you asked them to punch you out. Take, for example, me and Clint. It would take so long to explain why he should hit me that it wouldn't be worthwhile. I would probably have already gone stark raving crazy by then.

Of course, then maybe he really would hit me because I was so crazy, but what's the use of it then?

June 26

We're coming into California now. I have seen my first palm tree. Everything is shimmering here, and it's hard to breathe. I think San Francisco is just a couple of hours west of here. There is a big airport there. I really need to get to that airport, but it's a long flight across the country. It was a mistake to come on this trip. I won't be able to survive out here. I can't breathe. We're driving too fast. Things are kind of dark at the edges. I've got to tell Clint to exit here and drive west. Is that the ocean I see over there? It can't be too far away—just a couple of hours. Maybe my parents could meet me in Nebraska. Maybe we could both take planes that arrive at the same time in Nebraska. No, I've got to get back to New Jersey. We can find a phone after we exit, and I can call my parents and ask them to come get me on the next plane. They will wonder why. "Oh, surely you're alright, dear," they will say. "Just take a deep breath, and you'll be fine." Yes, my mother would stay very calm and tell me to take a deep breath. She doesn't know. But she will be very sad when I have gone crazy. "Who would have ever guessed?" people will say. My parents will shake their heads. My mother will dab a handkerchief to her eye in church on Sunday and say, "She always was a sensitive child." But she will know that people will be wondering what was wrong with Lucille and George that their daughter went crazy. They will wonder what they didn't give me. They will wonder why they didn't take better care of me.

Clint did not turn off at that exit. We are getting farther and farther away from the airport.

Maybe I should talk to Clint about hitting me if I asked him to.

As we traveled through the country, I didn't tell Rick the extent of my anxiety. He recalled me studying maps and being quiet for long periods but had no idea what was happening in my head. I never shared the scope of my fears with anyone—the most I'd say was that I was uncomfortable somewhere or preferred not to do something, but I never told them the truth. How could I explain the irrational degree to which I detached? Or describe my feelings of disintegration? Even if I could find the words, people would think I was insane.

Rick's first experience of being affected by my anxiety came during that cross-country trip. It happened as we were driving across northeast Wyoming on a beautiful June day with a wide-open sky and a soft wind that smelled of hay. Rick turned off Interstate 90 and followed a two-lane highway looking for an inspiring vista, while I nervously checked the map to ensure this highway would rejoin the interstate ahead. After driving along the winding road a distance, Rick noticed the sign for a scenic rest stop and pulled over. There was an empty picnic table perched on a ledge that overlooked a lifeless, lunar landscape with nothing from one horizon to the next but rock plateaus and shallow canyons, a swath of gray with hard black shadows and nothing but wilderness stretching as far as we could see.

The wind was warm and dry, its hollow moan the only sound. This was the most desolate, forgotten place I'd ever been, and it evoked every feeling of abandonment and disconnection in me. I couldn't wait to leave. As my anxiety ramped up, Rick was rummaging through the car and emerged carrying the watermelon we'd bought at our last grocery stop. He placed it on the picnic table with paper towels and a large knife.

"What are you doing?" I asked.

He looked at me with surprise, "Let's have the watermelon! Isn't this a terrific spot?" The watermelon glistened in the sun, beads of sweat running down the bright green rind onto the rough wooden table.

I wanted to run screaming from this place, and he wanted to have a picnic here? "*This* place?" My voice cracked.

Rick picked up the knife to slice into the juicy fruit and stopped. He looked at me with bewilderment as I grabbed his arm and dragged him back to the car, "No, no, not here!" I shouted, jumping into the car and pulling the door closed. Rick stood there, confused. I turned my head to speak through the window. "I don't like this place at all," I said. "We need to get out of here!" Ashamed of my behavior but feeling more unglued by the minute, I was trying to stave off a complete and absolute panic attack. This was not the time or place for an explanation; we just had to get out of there.

He could tell I was serious. Something had me rattled, and he reluctantly put the watermelon back in the car and climbed into the driver's seat. My head was lowered. I was looking over the map, avoiding the unsettling view, and searching for a route away from this forsaken spot, but I knew he was looking at me. Rick chuckles whenever he tells the story. "I couldn't understand the problem. I thought it was a terrific place for a picnic. But you freaked out!" He shakes his head with endearment. While he now understands the terror it triggered in me, he still gave me unquestioning support back then.

I had hoped to keep my dark fears to myself, but the trip across the county pushed me to my limits, and I had to confess the enormity of my anxiety to Rick. I was so ashamed, but if we were going to build a life together, he needed to know these things about me. My anxiety made me feel "less than" and damaged, and I worried they'd cause Rick to reject me. Who'd want to be with me if I interfered with their freedom and adventure?

Thankfully, Rick didn't consider my fears a deal breaker, and he proposed to me in the middle of a beautiful stream in the Uinta Mountains while visiting his family in Salt Lake City. We planned a simple streamside ceremony in the spirit of popular bohemian weddings, viewing our marriage as personal and private. A remote, nontraditional wedding was also an opportunity for me to declare independence from my home and family, yet I knew it didn't feel right after a few days of planning.

Rick and I realized we wanted to celebrate our marriage with all our family and friends, so I called my parents and asked if we could plan a traditional wedding in New Jersey, and they were thrilled. My brother Eric later told me they were upset by the prospect of my getting married without them, and they had looked into flights to Salt Lake City to be with us at our intended streamside nuptials. For some reason, I was surprised they cared that much. Rick and I were casual about wedding traditions, and neither of us had appreciated what the ceremony represented to our families. After deciding on a formal wedding, we picked a date at the end of the summer. We couldn't understand why anyone needed a whole year to organize such an event, so staying flexible on just about every detail, we managed to pull ours together in just two months, engraved invitations included. We were married in late August at my childhood church in New Jersey.

The morning of the ceremony was hectic and rushed in the red-brick house where I grew up. The photographer gathered my family and the bridesmaids together, and one of my favorite pictures is of me looking out over the lake through the big picture window in the living room. Once the pre-wedding photos were taken, it was time to leave for the church, and everyone spilled out onto the front lawn to find their ride. I went to check my makeup and returned to the living room to find the house still and the yard empty. At least my sister, Susie, my maid of honor, was in the kitchen. "Where'd everyone go?"

She looked at me unconcerned, "I guess they all went to the church. How are we getting there?"

I shook my head in disbelief. "They forgot the bride and the maid of honor?"

Peering out the kitchen window, I hoped to see a car in the driveway to drive myself and Susie to my wedding, but none was there.

Nor was there a way to call anyone at the church. There weren't cell phones then.

"Well," I quipped, "they're bound to miss us at some point."

We walked back to the living room and stood before the picture window, holding our bouquets like mannequins dressed for a pretend wedding. I was a bride, forgotten at home on my wedding day.

After what felt like a long time, Dad sheepishly appeared to retrieve us, without explanation or even an anecdote about when they figured it out. Still annoyed, we trailed across the front lawn and climbed into Dad's Buick. It was challenging to de-puff our full gowns and fit through the car door, but bouquets in one hand and tucking with the other, we slid across the back seat. There was nothing glamorous about my arrival at the church, but the ceremony went beautifully once there.

As Dad and I stood at the entrance waiting for the procession to begin, he took my arm and held on to it. My very favorite photo of the day is a picture of Dad and me just before we stepped forward. I'm looking straight ahead, smiling, and Dad has a wistful half smile and a very faraway look in his eyes.

I've always been glad we'd chosen to have a larger, more formal wedding, though I peppered it with several nontraditional details. Rick and I exchanged vows we'd written ourselves, and it was important to us to have the reception outside in a garden, with only classical guitar music. We celebrated with a luncheon for one hundred fifty guests on the outdoor balcony of a historic estate, setting tables with white linen between the immense stone pillars. Formal gardens with clipped beds and gravel paths spread out below, and a center fountain splashed cool water through the late August afternoon. A dear friend sang our chosen song for us, and despite the grand setting, the mood was casual and conversational. We could be in the moment with our friends and families and thought it was perfect.

CHAPTER THIRTEEN

Loved Ones in Need

1978, 1989, 2010

Immediately after the wedding, we returned to Los Angeles, our jobs too new to allow us time for a honeymoon. As we settled into our California life, it became clear that our trip across the country, the wedding, and the stress of living in a completely new environment had taken a toll on me. Though I appeared perfectly normal as I worked and socialized, I was phobic about being alone. Not in all situations, but in any unfamiliar setting or when driving alone, my center would disappear.

The dissolution in those situations was so intense I couldn't fathom why everyone else didn't feel that way. Was I really the only one who had these overwhelming fears? Was I *that* crazy? Rick traveled extensively for his job, and I asked him if he'd ever felt untethered and frighteningly alone while on the road, but he couldn't even grasp the concept. "No," he replied. "Wherever I go, there I am! I'm always me!"

Maybe that was my problem. There wasn't enough "me" to begin with.

In 1979, there was no shortage of self-enlightenment groups in California, and some of the partners at Rick's financial firm touted the benefits of one particular organization. We decided it would be interesting to join a weekend seminar and headed up the coast to Northern California.

Winding our way through steep hills, heavily wooded with pine trees, we checked in at the camp, where mornings were misty and cool and afternoons hot and dry. The raw wood cabins were the color of honey and smelled of sun-warmed cedar, and we walked the property on fern-lined paths. The group included friendly professionals of various ages and we attended interesting lectures and gathered for communal meals in the bright dining hall.

On the last afternoon, Rick and I caught the closing lecture. We sat in a circle of folding chairs surrounded by bulletin boards with colorful announcements scattered all over them. High beamed ceilings held a sunny cupula, and windows around the room revealed the bright blue sky, paths of ochre earth, and the rough, brown bark of pine trees. We were instructed to get comfortable, to sit or lie anywhere, and to listen to the music. Rick and I chose to lie on the floor. Once we were in place, I shut my eyes and tuned into the music. Pachelbel's "Canon in D" was playing, a popular recording that year, and I let my mind drift with the familiar rise and fall of the composition. While listening to the music, we were instructed to think about our mothers and something we'd like to say to them but never had.

I pictured Mom while rewinding my life and tried to attach words to feelings, but nothing initially sprang to mind. I couldn't seem to hold on to an image of her or think of anything to say, even when I ran through the obvious disappointments and hurts. They just didn't stick; they felt flimsy and obvious. The music soared and swelled while I waited for my mind to settle on something, when suddenly, I was overcome. Something unexpected erupted at my core, and a mournful cry wailed out of me. I tried to gulp it down, but it couldn't be suppressed. I began to sob—wrenching, racking, heaving sobs that took my breath away. They were so primal and violent, like a punch to the stomach, that I physically folded in on myself, wrapping my arms around my waist. Tears streamed down my face, copious and unstoppable, running into my mouth as my breathing grew more ragged. I lost complete control of myself. Whatever this was came from deep down in my gut and felt very specific. Weeping seemed the only way it could be released, and I couldn't stop. Embarrassed, I ran out of the building in tears, and though none of the counselors followed, Rick was there in a minute with his arms around me.

The only way to describe my feelings is "profound grief." I didn't know it was possible to hold feelings so deeply, in fathoms I couldn't even imagine. Nor was I aware of any particular thought about my mother to have triggered such a violent reaction. I never understood what happened to me that day until many years later when my therapist suggested I was sobbing for two mothers—the one I'd once lost at birth and the one who'd raised me. The moment he spoke those words they reached inside and unlatched my grief again. It floated up and curled through me. It was so familiar, I knew it had always been there, and now it was within reach, just below my skin, pushing against me like light trying to escape.

There were powerful feelings I had never acknowledged, and so much I didn't understand. Therapy would be critical on the journey to finding and freeing myself. At this point there was still a long way to go, but I was awakening, and strengthening, for all that was to come.

We lived in Los Angeles for two years, where I found administrative jobs, first at USC and then at UCLA. Neither position had anything to do with my education or interests, but holding a BA in fine arts and literature was not exactly a hot ticket for employment in LA in 1978. I didn't like Los Angeles, an irrigated city in the desert. I missed cool, rainy days that begged you to stay inside with a good book and bake cookies. I missed autumn leaves and lilacs, and never got used to Christmas shopping in shorts. Colleagues would say, "Oh, Janet, you're so East Coast!" which I knew wasn't a compliment, but I took it as one. Never, in those two years, did I consider Los Angeles my home, and I was ecstatic when Rick accepted a job with an investment bank on Wall Street, and we moved back to New York at the end of 1980.

One of the best things about moving back East was finding a therapist who specialized in anxiety. Dr. VanAmberg spent his career studying panic attacks after suffering from them himself and devoted his practice to helping patients manage anxiety. He explained what a panic attack was, why it happened, and the symptoms it caused. I finally understood I wasn't dying or going crazy. My body was reacting to excess adrenaline, which wreaked havoc with my physiology. Dr. VanAmberg assured me I could manage the adrenaline surges and prescribed as-needed doses of a beta-blocker. If I felt a panic attack coming on, I could stop it in its tracks with the medication. Working with Dr. VanAmberg freed me from the horrific attacks that plagued me since I was a child and allowed me to finally manage my anxiety with normal, appropriate responses.

Meanwhile, we purchased our first home in Short Hills, New Jersey, after Rick took the train out of the city and decided that was as far as he wanted to commute. Rick was with a "Big Eight" accounting firm in Los Angeles, and I was used to him working long hours, but they paled compared to the hours he worked on Wall Street. His usual daily commute from Short Hills began on the 5:50 a.m. train into New York and ended with him returning home around 8:30 p.m. He was at his desk in his home office on weekends—part of the day on Saturday, and all day on Sunday. He traveled such a great deal that he was away on business as much as he was at home. Some spouses didn't do well with such a schedule, but it worked both personally and professionally for me.

At the time, I ran a home-based business creating intricate felt Christmas stockings. The Gazebo, then a well-known Madison Avenue boutique, sold my creations in their New York City, Dallas, and Beverly Hills stores and ordered hundreds of stockings every year. Each of the six designs I made was like a painting created in felt with three-dimensional details. In the holiday scenes they depicted, rugs were braided, curtains were gathered, and tiny satin bows adorned children's hair. This level of specificity required an ambitious production schedule, and since I couldn't find a way to outsource the precise work, I produced the greater part of each stocking myself. When I wasn't hunched over a Christmas stocking or working on a house project, I spent my time reading, writing, or painting. These solitary endeavors kept me busy and fulfilled, and Rick's consuming work gave me plenty of time to pursue my interests.

Though I was often physically alone, Rick and I were in touch throughout the day by phone. Despite his absence, I felt connected to him and was surprised one day to discover the neighbors thought I was a single woman, since they rarely saw Rick coming or going.

Most of the couples in our community had young children, and the moms mingled on front lawns as kids roamed from yard to yard. Even though I didn't have children, I joined in and got to know my Whitney Road neighbors standing among Maclaren strollers, Big Wheels, and more children than I could count.

One of the young mothers in the children's play group lived directly across the street, and we became fast friends. Janie would often invite me in for coffee when the play group paused for naps, and

I was impressed with the chintz-skirted tables and original oil paintings in her lovely Tudor home. She was smart, beautiful, and stylish. She didn't think twice about adding a gold brooch to the shoulder of a T-shirt with jeans. More chic than the other moms, Janie had that fashion *je ne sais quoi*. It was so subtle you couldn't quite figure out why, but she always looked cool. She knew something about everything, was funny and caring, and became a cherished confidante. Her one-year-old daughter, Ann, was full of energy and curiosity, and I got such a kick out of her. When we first met, Janie was expecting her second child and I enjoyed helping however I could. When baby Lloyd was born, two-year-old Ann spent extra time at my house. She showed me her favorite Mister Rogers shows, and I shared my favorite Fred Astaire and Bing Crosby movies with her. Ann was the only child in the neighborhood who whistled "The Continental" or "Cheek to Cheek" as she danced and played, and she was convinced that Rick and I would name our first child Fred Bing Sherlund. We looked forward to having children but were waiting for the moment to feel right, and in 1985, it did.

Our first child was due in March of 1986, and I was thrilled to think I'd finally have a blood connection in this world. When Will was born, the first thing everyone said was how he looked just like Rick! I'd remind them that I was a part of the equation, but it was hard to see any resemblance to me in the baby I held. Though my DNA was not apparent in baby Will, he came to look much more like me in adolescence. Conversely, when our second son, Ben, was born in 1989, he looked like me but became a clone of Rick in adolescence. I cherished any similarities with the boys. They were the first blood I ever shared, and I was hungry to see myself in them. I loved them fiercely and was happy to be a full-time stay-at-home mom.

As we watched the boys grow up, I wondered about the missing pieces of the puzzle. We recognized the traits they shared with Rick's family, but what about mine? Were there medical issues we needed to know about, risks to mitigate? Every doctor's appointment had forms I couldn't complete—all the questions about family history were passed over as I scrawled "Adopted" across the page. I didn't like being an unknown factor for my children, offering nothing beyond myself. Where did I come from? Where did *we* come from?

"We should hire a private detective to locate your birth mother," Rick said. "Someone has got to be able to find her!"

But we had nothing to work with. My adoption agency had given me all they could legally share, the adoption reunion registry hadn't provided any results, and my birth records were tightly sealed in New Jersey. We had no names and no place of origin, and this was decades before DNA websites existed. I read everything I could find about adoption and drilled down into news stories about reunions. I looked at every face I passed, wondering if that person might be related to me. But after a lifetime of no information and no leads, it all became normalized. The feeling of loss and the black hole in my gut were as much a part of me as my blue eyes. I integrated my sorrow like grief integrates into a mourner's life—you never get "over" your loss. It's not forgotten; you just learn to live with it.

Meanwhile, I was busy with the boys' activities and took parent leadership roles in their schools. Together, Rick and I tackled learning disabilities, ADD, and the challenges of adolescence. Both boys faced hurdles as they grew up, but each found their stride, and we couldn't be prouder of the young men they grew to be. During these years, I also served on nonprofit community boards and managed our New Jersey home and the summer home we bought on Nantucket while Rick continued his demanding work and travel schedule. My adoptive family required more attention as we aged. My parents, as well as my siblings and their married families, needed additional emotional and financial support. Between it all, I was utterly spent and the big black hole inside me had to wait. I kept going, pushing all my feelings down as far as they would go.

In 2007 Rick retired from the investment firm where he was a partner, and anticipating a new, noncommuting lifestyle, we moved to rural New Jersey in 2008. Rick's plan to work from home and enjoy the natural beauty of our surroundings didn't last long, and he eventually resumed his commute to the city. We were now in our fifties, the boys were out of the house, Rick was still working long hours, and we lived in a new town where we didn't know many people. Luckily, I loved the solitude and peace of the country and settled comfortably into our new life.

We still enjoyed our closest friends. Happily, Janie and her husband, Jeff, didn't live far from our new home, and my friends Nancy and Diane and their husbands (whom we'd come to know through my nonprofit work) remained dear friends. Other friends were moving on to "second chapters," spreading out across the country, and it was challenging to get together. With fewer social demands, I turned my attention to interests I'd set aside. This included finally trying to solve the mystery of who I was.

While chatting on the phone with Mom one day, I asked what happened to our adoption agency. I hadn't heard it mentioned in years and assumed it closed. To my surprise, Mom told me it was still open, and they even had a website.

As soon as I hung up with Mom, I typed the agency's name on my keyboard, and it popped up on my screen. Clicking on their home page, I scanned the options and saw a tab with the word "Search." I clicked on it, and my heart nearly stopped.

In 1980 my adoption agency began a program of uniting birth parents and adoptees. By paying a $650 fee and completing an application and an in-person interview, they would conduct a search and connect the birth parent and adoptee if both were agreeable. They had been doing this for over thirty years, starting just three years after my inquiry when I graduated from college. I couldn't believe this had been happening all these years and I'd never known! After I received the letter they sent in 1977, I thought there was nothing more they could or would do. The idea of the agency facilitating reunions was beyond my wildest dreams!

I filled out the form and prayed my birth mother was still alive. Because they held all her identifying information, I was sure they'd be able to locate her, if it wasn't too late. The agency acknowledged my application, telling me that it could take nine months before they processed my paperwork, given the number of inquiries already in the queue. I adjusted my expectations and tried to quell my lifelong curiosity.

A few months later, my younger brother, Mark, called with shocking news. "Janet, Eric had a stroke and is being airlifted to a hospital."

Eric had a stroke? Our thin, fit, healthy, fifty-seven-year-old brother? A stroke? I grabbed the counter and tried to steady myself. What was happening? Where was he?

Eric suffered a massive brain bleed and was in a neuroscience intensive care unit in Pennsylvania, about an hour and a half from where I lived in New Jersey. The bleeding was at the brainstem and resulted in profound damage. The cause was untreated high blood pressure, the silent killer Eric had unwittingly inherited.

Eric's wife, Gail, was devastated though she didn't yet know how Eric's care would consume her life from that moment on. It was difficult enough to process the catastrophic change to her previously strong, active husband and deal with medical bills totaling over a million dollars. Eric needed round-the-clock care when he was discharged from rehab three months later, and Gail was determined to tend to him at home, which she did with unwavering dedication. I tried to support her however I could, which was often by simply being there to talk.

Eric had always come through for me in meaningful ways, especially at difficult times, and I wanted to be there for him in whatever way possible. When we were kids, Eric was a terrible tease, and in high school, he tormented me (he thought I was too shy and bookish). We were as different as can be, but he grew up to be a thoughtful and caring brother whom I loved very much. Eric was the other sibling who helped most with Mom and Dad in their later years, anticipating their needs, installing a generator for their house, or building a bench on their beach so they didn't have to lug chairs up and down the hill. While I took care of Mom and Dad's day-to-day requirements, since they lived only twenty minutes from me, Eric was always available and eager to assist, often in big ways. He was happy to help anyone, anytime, and when I was in college, he did something for me that was one of the most selfless acts I'd ever experienced.

The week before graduation from Colgate, I was lonely and scared. Devastated by the recent breakup with Lonny and feeling at loose ends, I was unsure about life after college. I remained on the ghostly campus, largely empty since underclassmen were now gone and most seniors were away for a short vacation before our graduation ceremony. While doing my best to be strong, I felt abandoned and was falling apart, panic taking hold once again. I didn't want to call my parents, so I dialed Eric's number. He was married and had two small sons, and I thought checking in with them would provide some distraction. There were always cute stories with little ones in the house. But the minute he picked up the phone, I burst into tears.

"Hold on," he said. "I'm coming to get you." And just like that, he jumped into his car and drove four and a half hours to pick me up. I don't remember what we talked about on the long drive back to his house, but I felt cared for and protected and enjoyed the week before graduation at his home with my laughing and tumbling nephews. It was just what I needed.

———

Eric's stroke was brutal for my elderly parents. It added an acutely emotional layer of stress onto their shrinking world, and they needed more care and attention in its aftermath. In the beginning, I drove them two hours to and from the hospital for daily visits with Eric, but those long and challenging days took a toll. Even when they decided to visit less often, the constant fear and worry remained, and they leaned on me more than ever—life had changed for us all.

Two weeks after Eric's stroke, the call came from my adoption agency asking me to come in for my search interview, but I simply couldn't. "Please move me back to the bottom of the pile. I am overwhelmed with a family emergency, and I can't take on something this deeply emotional."

It was the right decision at the time but a difficult one to make. My adoptive family was falling apart, and between Eric's debilitating stroke and Mom and Dad's increasing frailty, I wanted to be there for them as much as possible. While this family always felt disconnected and borrowed, it was the only one I knew. They were my base—I needed them—and the idea of finding my birth mother now felt like it might topple the only family I'd ever known.

Of course, I, the good child, would continue my role as the caretaker and put aside any thoughts of my own growth and needs as my adoptive family faced this crisis. Security was more important to me than discovery. I'd waited this long in life. I could wait longer.

Nine months later, the adoption agency called again and invited me to come in for my interview. While I didn't feel ready to move forward, they told me if I didn't come, they would revoke my application, and I'd have to reapply at a future date. Eric was then as stable as he could be, and the family was getting used to the new normal. There was no reason I couldn't proceed.

Though a year earlier I'd been eager to start my search, now I wasn't so sure. After all we'd been through, I was emotionally exhausted and protective of my adoptive family. I was also skeptical about whether the search would be successful and afraid it was too late for a reunion. I was sure something would go wrong and didn't know if I could handle that. I was fifty-six years old, and it seemed life had other things in store for me, but in the end, I heard myself say, "Okay, I'll come in for my interview next week."

CHAPTER FOURTEEN

First Contact

2010–2011

The adoption agency was in a typical modern office building, not the stately old house I remembered when my parents adopted my baby sister. The downstairs offices were small and dark, with tight rows of desks and file cabinets. The lack of light surprised me, but when the social worker in charge of searches, Gloria, greeted me, her bright smile invited me in.

Gloria had been at the agency for many years and knew of my adoptive parents and siblings, so our conversation felt more social than interrogative. The interview wasn't as formal as I expected. It seemed the agency only wanted to make sure I wasn't crazy and could handle the search process. She knew about the "Adoption and Identity" paper I had written in college and the letter the agency sent to me in 1977. We discussed issues that could arise in a search—nothing that alarmed me—and we reviewed a folder of articles and a reading list. I'd already read many of the books cited, but there was a lot of new information in the folder, many reprinted articles, and I welcomed all of it. She shared some inspiring reunion stories from the agency, one of a famous television actor and his daughter, as well as searches with disappointing endings. I loved hearing how searches changed people's lives, whether by bringing a relationship to life or offering closure. Gloria did a good job of encouraging me while tempering expectations. There were no promises, even with all the information they had from my original adoption fifty-six years earlier. First, they had to find my birth mother. Then she had to agree. There were still a lot of ifs.

I left the interview steeled for disappointment. Despite the agency's success rate, I wasn't convinced my search would work. It had been so long. My birth mom would be seventy-five, if she was still alive. Had it been too long?

To my astonishment, they found her within the week! Gloria called with the news that she was alive and well, and they knew how to reach her. However, before contacting her, they needed a letter from me describing who I was, why I wanted to meet her, and what my life had been like. Gloria told me I should address her by her first name, Shirlie, spelled with an "ie," and that I should include photographs of myself as a baby, child, and adult. When complete, I should send it to Gloria for approval, and they would make contact and ask if she'd be willing to receive it.

I was thrilled! I wanted to shout from the rooftops! How lucky was I? My mother was alive and well! What did she look like? Did we have features in common? What interests did we share? I wondered what it would feel like to look into my mother's eyes—after fifty-six years, I was finally going to meet my mother! I hoped she'd be proud of the woman I'd become, and I couldn't wait to feel her arms around me.

Buzzed with excitement, my brain couldn't settle. It took a few days to compose the letter. Writing to the mother I'd yearned for every day of my life was daunting. When the words came, they arrived in a rush. In addition to the details of my life, I gently described what it felt like to be adopted and said I understood my birth hadn't been a welcome event in her life, and I respected her desire to keep this private. Assuring her I didn't need anything material from her, I asked only that she'd consider speaking with me.

My letter passed the agency's scrutiny, was mailed, and the wait began. I tried to put it out of my mind and distract myself in every way possible, but it was with me in every heartbeat.

Before another week passed, Gloria called to tell me she had spoken with Shirlie. The world stopped while I held my breath and leaned into Gloria's words, eager to know every detail. I was stunned to hear Shirlie described as emotionally reluctant and concerned with her reputation, telling Gloria the pregnancy didn't reflect well on her. Shirlie said it would be an embarrassment to her husband and children, who didn't know about me, and no, she wouldn't meet me.

"Janet is a lovely and accomplished person," Gloria pressed.

"I wouldn't expect anything different," said the woman who, fifty-six years earlier, told another social worker that I wasn't "even real" to her.

I couldn't comprehend her response. She was seventy-five years old, had five other children, was in her second marriage, and hadn't lived in her hometown for fifty-six years! She worked outside the home; it would be easy to meet for coffee or lunch. No one would have to know who I was, but she didn't want to meet me. She had expelled me from her body and extinguished me from her life. How dare she take credit for my being lovely and accomplished!

Her denial was wrenching, and my center twisted into a knot so tight I went numb.

You can't deny me again, I thought.

But she had.

Questions looped through my brain—why don't you want to meet me? Can I mean that little? Didn't you ever wonder about me?

Wouldn't you like to at least see me? I'm a nice person. I think you would be proud. *Why don't you want to meet me?*

In *The Primal Wound*, Nancy Newton Verrier writes, "Sometimes the adoptee experiences a second rejection upon making contact with his birth mother . . . being rejected again is devastating for the adoptee. . . . All the excruciating feelings of abandonment and loss . . . resurface."

With her outright rejection, something in me broke. I curled into the deep cushions in the family room and pulled a blanket over myself. The fireplace was lit, the room smelled of raw wood and smoke, and the television saturated the room with an electronic drone. I have no memory of leaving the sofa for a very long time—weeks, maybe a month. I stared out the window at the dulling season. The sky went gray, the woods turned hard, and the grass browned. At some point, my husband and sons moved in and out of the background as the Christmas tree went up and the lights were strung, the multicolored ones that reminded me of my childhood Christmases. They hung the hundreds of ornaments I'd collected, but to no effect. Snow fell, drifting in slow motion past the window as I sat empty, confused, and helpless.

I didn't cry, though I was devastated. I felt I might suffocate—that this blow could extinguish me. In those moments, defending myself against that awful feeling, I told myself I shouldn't take this so hard. I was a grown fifty-six-year-old woman! But I couldn't protect myself against emotions I didn't understand. I was feeling something deeper and more profound than I knew: something somatic, preverbal, and unconscious.

It was something from deep down in a place I didn't have words for. A trauma from before I had language, from a time when terror could be expressed only in wailing and shrieks and gulping sobs alone in a crib: flailing arms, a red face, a burning throat of fear from having been abandoned. For nine months, I heard my mother's voice, felt her rhythms, and tasted her. We were bonded physically and emotionally. I came from that woman's body. I shared her DNA. I had been one with her until I suddenly was not. When those bonds were severed, there was a profound loss. I was crying in a nursery, and I was alone.

Now I felt like I'd been abandoned again. The primal wound had not healed.

Ninety-six percent of birth mothers want to meet the child they gave up, even a child conceived from rape. But not mine. She had no concern for my needs, only her own.

I was not important. I was not wanted. I was, frankly, not even real.

The agency was appalled. Her refusal surprised them, and they went back to read the notes from 1954 when she placed me for adoption. The social worker who interviewed Shirlie at the time made note of her extraordinary denial, something they rarely, if ever, saw in birth mothers. That characteristic hadn't been revealed in their 1977 letter to me, but it helped me to hear it now. Something was off about this woman, my birth mother.

Gloria told me they had my birth father's name and asked if I wanted them to contact him. That was a question I wasn't prepared for. My birth father didn't know I existed. His consent wasn't required in 1954, and my birth mother never told him about her pregnancy. I knew that much from the 1977 letter the agency sent. Would I feel connected to a seventy-five-year-old man who had no idea I existed? It was my birth mother I'd yearned and searched for. I hadn't given much thought to the man who'd contributed 50 percent of my DNA. Yet realizing he might have important medical information for my sons and me, I begrudgingly agreed to try to find him.

It didn't take long for Gloria to track him down. He was still living in the town he'd grown up in, where he and Shirlie had gone to school. Gloria reached him by phone while he was watching *Jeopardy*, and he was shocked to learn he had a daughter with his high school sweetheart. He asked Gloria to call him again the next night. First he wanted to do two things: confirm the agency was legit and call Shirlie to ask her if it was true. Shirlie's phone number was listed on a recent high school reunion roster, and he called immediately, but she hung up on him without answering his question. However, the agency did check out, and when Gloria called him back the next night, his response was, "If she has my blood, she is my daughter. Of course, I want to meet her."

The agency asked me to write a second letter, to a man named Larry, my birth father. They forwarded the letter to him, and I waited for the second time in as many months.

This time Gloria called me with good news. Larry would like to meet me. She gave me basic information about him: He was a retired New York State Trooper, a widower, and had three grown children. She suggested we meet at a neutral, public place between our homes as soon as possible.

She also told me she'd received an angry phone call from Shirlie, who believed her rights from fifty-six years ago should supersede my right to know anything about my birth father.

There was no turning back now. Contact had been made. People knew about me. *Family* knew about me. The birth father I'd never thought about knew I existed and wanted to meet me. It wasn't anything I'd ever imagined, and the surreal feeling made me wonder if this was moving too fast. Why the rush? How could I go from knowing nothing about this man to becoming a part of his family? I'd set something in motion I could no longer control.

Larry called me a few days later, on a December evening, to make initial contact and find a date to meet. He told me his grown children gasped when they saw my photos. I looked so much like them one of my half sisters wondered how I'd gotten ahold of "her" baby pictures.

I remember my conversation with Larry as charged with excitement, all nerves and laughter, not too personal or profound, just happy and pleasant. Since I hadn't spent my life wondering about this man, I didn't have expectations or preconceived notions. I didn't think meeting him would be life-changing but thought it might be interesting. However, after our phone call, I was consumed by curiosity and impatience. I wanted to know everything *now*. I wanted to see pictures and learn more about all of them. Our meeting wouldn't occur until weeks after Christmas, and I didn't think I could stand it. I googled him but found nothing. How could this man not have any online presence? Left with only my anxiety-driven imagination, I was a complete wreck by the time we got to our planned meeting date, January 8, 2011.

CHAPTER FIFTEEN

Flesh and Blood
2011

It was a gray, snowy Saturday. The kind of day that, exhausted from the holidays and depressed by the weather, I'd rather have stayed in bed and pulled the covers over my head. But today was the day I would fulfill my lifelong dream of meeting my origins. Agitated and unsettled, I tried on too many outfits, searching for just the right one, and was teary and upset that all my jeans felt tight. I finally settled into the least snug pair and added a favorite shirt and sweater.

Rick and I were to meet Larry and two of my half siblings, Sean and Jessica, at a resort about an hour from our home. I nestled into the car, feeling fragile and unsure, as Rick slid behind the wheel. The world slipped by my window, dim and streaky, and with each passing mile, my courage faded more. Was the reason my father didn't have an online presence because he lived off the grid, in a trailer, and was three hundred pounds, with stained sweatpants and long, greasy hair? This didn't align with anything I knew about Larry. I was simply terrified as we barreled up the New York State Thruway toward my destiny.

When we arrived at the resort, my rubbery legs barely crossed the parking lot into the lobby. The building was larger than I'd imagined, and I had no idea where the restaurant was or how Larry and I would recognize each other. I should have suggested something—flowers pinned to our lapels or a particular colored shirt. Sweat pricked across my brow and down my spine. I pulled off my heavy coat and clutched it like a life preserver.

Discouraged and confused, I withdrew while Rick remained on high alert. He scanned the area and spied an older man on a bench across the lobby. When they locked eyes, he knew immediately it was Larry. Rick didn't say a thing as the man stood and walked toward us. I was looking the other way and still oblivious.

Suddenly, someone was standing in front of me, and I felt his hands fold over mine, saw his face lean close, a face that was wide and open with bright blue eyes. He held on firmly, looked directly into my eyes, and said, "You're Janet."

I wasn't prepared for the connection, to see myself in his eyes, his face. I wasn't prepared for the lifelong hole in my gut to slam shut the moment he took my hands in his, smiled, and said those two simple words: "You're Janet."

I was found.

I looked into my father's eyes, and I finally made sense.

Like magnet to iron. I imagined two objects pulling together. The hard edges made contact—a powerful, smooth connection. They fit. Perfectly. I felt it right in my gut—the hollow space inside filling up. This was the missing piece. So smooth and tight was the connection that "magnet to iron" was the only way to describe it. A magnet that slid perfectly into a deep, oiled cylinder and fused. I've never used those words before or seen those images. The emptiness had always felt rough-hewn and jagged, but now the edges felt hard-polished and inextricably drawn together. It happened just like that. I was connected. The eyes. The nose. At long last.

There was a circle of people around us. My half brother, Sean; his wife, Gayle; and my half sister, Jessica. Everyone was crying. There was not a dry eye among us.

Larry placed a book in my hand, his high school yearbook. Perched on top was a name tag from a recent reunion, which had his senior photo imprinted on it. I gasped. He looked exactly like our firstborn son, Will. *Exactly.* Will was the spitting image of his grandfather. I was dumbfounded.

We moved, en masse, to a large corner table and remained for hours, talking and laughing and feeling so comfortable it was confusing. Larry and I couldn't take our eyes off each other. He said he saw so much of my mother in me it made him feel eighteen again. Occasionally, I was aware of Rick, Sean, Gayle, and Jessica staring at us, smiling, and though I couldn't hear what they were saying, Rick was having a great time with them. They were acting like . . . family. Later, Rick told me how much he loved watching me and Larry talk and how connected he felt with Sean, Gayle, and Jessica. He said he already embraced them as family and would do anything for them.

I wanted some answers about my biology, to see someone I looked like, but I never imagined it would be somatic—that the connection would be so molecular. Do cells have memory? Do we feel a connection that travels back through generations of flesh and blood? Do we recognize our kin in some primal way, like animals? I didn't know this man or this family, yet I felt as if I was welcomed home after wandering for a lifetime. I was back with my people, my clan. I stood with them. It was us against the world. How could these *strangers* feel like my most authentic family?

Thoughts of Larry consumed me for the first few weeks after meeting him. I wanted to see or talk to him all the time. It felt like falling in love. I'd send an email, worry about what I said—or didn't—and wonder if I was overwhelming him with too many messages. I checked my email constantly; he always responded quickly, and I devoured every word he wrote. Like a schoolgirl with a crush, I was giddy, in awe, and inexperienced. There was no precedent for this relationship, a grown child and parent meeting for the first time. Without baggage to complicate our relationship, it was fresh and pure. I was enthralled.

One night a few weeks later, I was restless and churning as Rick slept, so I decided to get up. Moonlight streamed through our large window and lay in crisp white on the carpet. As I moved through the light, my shadow appeared, sharp and eerily accurate. My bare feet stepped, my robe flapped, and the shadow mimicked every movement. But something was off that I couldn't quite figure out. I was relieved when the shadow faded in the darkened hall. But when I returned to the bedroom, my razor-sharp silhouette reappeared, and once again, it was disturbing.

Hearing Rick's slow, even breathing, I turned back to bed, where the moonlight washed across the comforter and childhood photos of the boys on the bedside table. As I pulled back the covers, I caught a glimpse of myself in the dressing table mirror and realized I looked just like Larry.

It was Larry I saw in my shadow. The shape of my body, arms, and posture was just like his. Until then, my shadow had been mine and mine alone, I'd never looked like anyone else. For fifty-six years, my reflection hadn't held any reference to another soul, but now I looked like someone else, someone I barely knew. There was history in my shapes and movements—other people owned them before me. I was built from their DNA. I was one of them, yet they were strangers to me.

I'd never again see myself without seeing someone else. Now I knew where I came from—but who were they? And who, after all, was I?

CHAPTER SIXTEEN

Heart and Soul
2011

Regular life resumed. The house looked ordinary without its Christmas finery. I answered emails and went to Pilates. Most dog walks took place in the dark, against biting wind. Mid-winter in New Jersey was dull and I was delighted to receive an invitation to lunch from my neighbor, Barbara, who always hosted a terrific mix of guests at her lovely home.

The aroma of bubbling cheese welcomed us, and a roaring fire chased the winter chill. Crystal and silver gleamed, and conversations skipped along, mixing easily between old friends and new. The light-hearted mood followed us to the table, where we raised our glasses, laughed, and chatted in the warm candleglow.

When we finished the first course, my friend Elaine and I cleared the dishes, and as we set them in the kitchen, she asked, "What's new?"

"Nothing," I replied. Then, just as the kitchen door opened and another woman walked in, I reconsidered my response. "Actually, I did just meet my biological father."

Elaine likely didn't know I was adopted, and I didn't know the other woman, so I was instantly embarrassed to have answered a basic question with such a personal response. But to my amazement, Elaine's eyes opened wide, and everything about her sprang to life. She leaned over the counter as the other woman turned, and they both begged to hear more. They seemed genuinely interested as I told my tale, as did others who happened into the kitchen. They hung on to every word, and I was impressed they were being so polite. I didn't think they could find all this so fascinating, and tried only to hit the highlights, not wanting to bore, but I could feel their excitement. They wanted to know everything!

After lunch, guests checked their watches and phones, and I went to gather my things, but Barbara stopped me. She'd heard about my story and insisted I couldn't leave before I told everyone! The women still at the table sat back in their chairs and looked at me expectantly. Cake crumbs and coffee cups were strewn over the white linen, the party was over, and I hesitated, unsure of their genuine interest until someone lifted a bottle of wine and filled empty glasses. Candles still dancing, I unwrapped my scarf, lowered myself into the nearest chair, and began. And they listened. To every word! They gasped and cheered, jumped up and asked me to repeat parts, and sat with tears in their eyes when I finished.

Why were they so interested? Wasn't this a story only adoptees would care about? I didn't understand, but I was happy to tell the tale.

Barbara told me she'd never seen me happier or more animated in the twenty-five years she'd known me. Did these new feelings show on my face and body? Had filling that big black hole transformed me in visible ways? It was the first time I shared my story publicly, and it surprised me that outsiders were drawn in. And for Barbara to tell me she'd never seen me happier in twenty-five years, well, that was astounding.

The changes *were* profound and deep. Repairing the primal wound, filling the gaping hole—it *was* magnet to iron. The relief, the connection, the completeness was something I'd never felt before. Meeting Larry filled the emptiness and created a bond that was astonishing and beyond my understanding. It happened in an instant, yet it seemed to burrow deep and occur on a cellular level. It was a molecular memory, a primal force that was staggering, a sense of belonging that was not a choice or a whim but an irrefutable fact. I could not stop smiling. I was radiating. I finally felt whole.

Of course, life never runs smoothly. Suddenly, there was a crisis with Dad, the father who raised me. He was sliding into cardiac failure but refusing surgery. Wary of doctors, Dad had been covering up his symptoms for years but now had trouble breathing and frequently lost his balance. Faced with the serious threat of losing him, my emotional connection shifted back to my "real" parents, the parents who raised me. All the hours I'd spent pursuing Larry and Shirlie felt like a betrayal, and I was consumed with guilt. Those hours could have been another afternoon at Mom and Dad's or more time chatting on the phone. Every minute directed away from them now felt wrong.

How long did Dad have? Would I have time to tell him how much I loved him—time to *show* him? Rick insisted my father knew, but faced with losing him, I wasn't sure. The quick, casual "Love you, Dad!" I said to him every day now seemed inadequate. Yet it was the limit of what he was comfortable with. Dad was Midwestern, of Scandinavian descent, reserved and undemonstrative, and he gave affection with a quick hug or a pat on the head. To say, "Dad, I love you so much. You were the parent who saved me, who made me feel love, who I admired more than anyone, and who I want to be like. Thank you for all the love you gave me. I will always love you," would have been too intimate for him. Sure, I said those things in birthday cards, where he could read them privately, but I never told him directly. Should I have? For my own peace of mind? Yes, I should have.

While I still wanted to see Larry, that didn't feel as urgent. He was so much younger than Dad, I assumed there'd be plenty of time. I also realized I needed to slow things down. I was trying to process too much, and it was more complicated than I had admitted.

My calm exterior belied a storm beneath. Pushed to my physical and emotional limits between being rejected by my birth mother, meeting my birth father, and facing my adopted father's life-threatening illness, I was rocked by waves of tachycardia severe enough to send me to the emergency room three times over the next two months. My doctor didn't find any physical problems with my heart, and I was forced to admit how profound these recent events were and remind myself to take a beat, slow down, and respect the power of everything I was experiencing. Intellectually I knew I should, but I was too overwhelmed to process those complicated emotions.

Dad was finally convinced he would die if he didn't have his heart valve replaced and agreed to the open-heart surgery. Given his otherwise good health, his surgeon was confident he'd survive, even at eighty-nine. Dad had one question—Would he be able to ski again? Surprised, the surgeon asked how recently he had skied. "Last winter," he replied, to which the surgeon laughed and said he saw no reason why he couldn't. They talked about what kind of heart valve to use, and Dad chose the cow valve, which could last twenty years. "I intend to wear it out," he chuckled.

While the surgery was successful, the recovery was complex, and Dad remained in the hospital for a month, during which time Mom came to live with Rick and me. She was a difficult guest who wanted help with dressing, demanded certain foods, expected assistance with emails and phone calls, and wanted to be chauffeured to many activities outside of hospital visits. Dad seemed like an incidental part of her day. While Mom always responded to stress with anger, criticism, and distraction, I thought this would be different. This was her husband, her beloved, and I expected her to behave like an attentive and loving wife, while I supported them in every way I could. Instead, she wore my patience thin.

Already frazzled by the recent events in my life, the challenge of living with Mom pushed me to the brink. I usually managed my relationship with her by regulating our time together. Our relationship worked in small doses, and I never imagined I'd have her living with me for any length of time. It was a very long, exhausting month.

When Dad was discharged from the hospital and they went home, it was a great relief. Caring for them returned to a less intensive pace, and I refocused on figuring out how to integrate the adopted me and the newly discovered biological me.

CHAPTER SEVENTEEN

A 'Sconset Gathering

2011–2012

In the summer of 2000, Rick and I decided to visit Nantucket, a small island thirty miles off Cape Cod, after hearing people describe the gardens, abundant roses, and mild summers. When Will and Ben were fourteen and eleven, we rented a house there, in the village of 'Sconset, and fell in love with the island. Before the summer was over, we'd purchased our own home on the 'Sconset bluff, and I recorded that day in my journal:

> We bought a house by the sea. It's a wonderful old gray gambrel and sits in the sunshine on a bluff overlooking the Atlantic Ocean in 'Sconset, on Nantucket. The yard is broad and open to the wind and light, and stretches down to the waves, with a white fence surrounding it that holds hydrangeas and roses. The light is intoxicating and addictive. I can't wait to return each time, feeling a physical need for it. I could be happy sitting in a lawn chair in the yard, just breathing.
>
> When I step back into New Jersey, I feel overwhelmed by the denseness and the claustrophobia of overhanging trees. I want to beat

them back and rip the sky open. On Nantucket, I saw the moon rising over the Atlantic as fresh and light as if it were suspended by magic, but when I stepped off the plane in New Jersey, the same moon felt veiled, muted, and sticky. I wanted to run back and felt as if I couldn't breathe. The world feels fresher on Nantucket.

And after a few summers in that home, I added these thoughts about 'Sconset:

I love the air and light and endless horizon of 'Sconset. The night sky is deep and dark with soft, humid air that brushes against your skin and wraps gently around you. The smell of the sea, roses, and wild honeysuckle mix and mingle, teasing and chasing each other from one moment to the next. The moon declares itself as large and as golden as possible, with moonbeams spreading across the dark water, scattering ever larger and wider as the waves move through them. The moonlight is alive with motion, waves running light and dark, light and dark as they tumble over each other toward the beach where they break with a quiet whoosh, like a lullaby. The soothing eternal rhythm makes you feel embraced and free at the same time.

'Sconset has the clearest, brightest blue days, with air so pure and charged with light it seems to shimmer around the edges. No matter the season, the light dazzles. January might fool you into thinking the day was mild, until you step out into the bluff wind that whips off the ocean with a dampness that moves through your core and out the other side as if there were no flesh around your bones, as if you were the cold air itself. But still, you go out, the light draws you to it.

In the evening, something magical happens at our arbor that stands before the beach. At the hour when the sun pauses low in the sky, molten and gold, it catches on the smooth arch, and the arbor becomes incandescent, reflecting whatever fire is left in the sun. When the sea has dulled and the sky merely a wash of yellow and rose, the arbor stands tall and luminous, glowing as it waits for the moon to rise behind.

The light on the arbor takes my breath away every time I see it. Perhaps it's the wonder of capturing the extraordinary light of 'Sconset. Perhaps the light, holding there in the dimming of the day, speaks to me of its power and promise. Perhaps the arbor, as it stands against the immense darkening horizon, reminds me I am standing on the edge of something mysterious and boundless. The light, the sky, and the sea at 'Sconset free my soul as nothing else can. They allow me to exhale, to breathe slow and deep, and to let my heart sing.

To me, there was nothing as personal or intimate as sharing Nantucket. It was my fondest wish to extend this part of my life to Larry, but my new siblings warned me that he didn't like to travel. I was thrilled when he surprised everyone and said he'd come! He flew to Nantucket by himself, settled into the guest house, and within days talked about staying all summer! Part of me wished he could, but another part was nervous about how this visit would go. Rick and our boys, now in their twenties, would be working off-island during most of Larry's visit, returning only on the weekends, as was the routine for working members of any family who summered on the island. Larry and I would be on our own most of the time, and I wondered if we'd be comfortable for such long stretches of uninterrupted time.

One of the first activities I planned was a tour of the Whaling Museum. I was the president of the board of the Nantucket Historical Association, which owns the museum, and the organization was very important to me.

Introducing Larry to my closest NHA colleagues and friends was the first time I'd introduced him to anyone. We stood in the vast Gosnell Hall, under the suspended bones of a massive whale skeleton. The museum had closed for the day, and the deep blue hall was quiet and still. A long, open whaleboat, filled with coiled ropes, tilted toward us, and iron whaling harpoons and captains' portraits lined the walls. It did feel odd to present this man, who I barely knew, as my father. Yet, as the words came out, something strong and true shot down my spine, and I stood a little taller.

The NHA staff looked forward to the premiere of their new gateway film, *Nantucket*, produced with legendary filmmaker Ric Burns. The movie was to be shown on a giant outdoor screen at Children's Beach on July 1, my fifty-seventh birthday. I was excited to have Larry with me but worried how he would manage alone while I fulfilled my president of the board duties, as Rick and the boys weren't due to arrive until after the premiere. Luckily our wonderful home property manager, Steven, was there with his family and introduced Larry to Nantucket Police Detective Tornavish. Larry and the detective quickly fell into conversation, and I headed off to make my remarks. When my duties were complete, I scanned the crowd for Larry to see him sitting in a circle with the detective and Steve, chatting with everyone around him as if they were old friends.

It was rather unbelievable but wonderful to have him with me on my birthday, a day he'd never been aware of. This felt like the first true birthday I'd ever had, as if all the ones before had been pretend. I felt real and grounded on my birthday for the first time ever, and now that Larry was with me, we could celebrate all the years we'd missed.

What I remember most about those first weeks with Larry was sitting by the pool under bluebird skies, talking all day. The air was fresh, the breeze smelled of the sea, and mounds of blue hydrangeas surrounded us. Sunshine dazzled on the turquoise water, and we talked about our lives and this unimaginable experience.

He told me again how much I looked like my birth mother, Shirlie, and how beautiful I was. I reminded him of the girl he loved at eighteen, who he remembered in all of her "Best Dressed," "Head Twirler," and "Miss High School" glory, and it made him feel young again. I leaned in to listen, eager and adoring, wanting to know everything about him. There was none of the sighing and eye-rolling a grown daughter might have for her father's too often repeated stories. They were all new to me. Every once in a while, I'd look at Larry and startle. Who was this man, and why do I feel so comfortable with him?

He would grow quiet at times, with a faraway look, and tell me he was thinking about all the moments he missed in my life. Imagining a Kodachrome slideshow of everything from my first steps to walking me down the aisle at my wedding, he fantasized about how he might have managed to raise me if only he knew I existed. He had a child he had never heard about. He had been robbed.

One day Larry's hand got caught as he was shutting the garden gate, and the injury was severe enough for the emergency room. We were there in minutes and waited to be called back to the examination room. When a nurse appeared and called his name, he stood, but I hesitated. Letting him go alone didn't feel right, but I wasn't sure if he'd feel comfortable with my coming. The nurse turned to me. "Are you family?" A tickle wiggled through my cheeks, and my face spread into a wide smile. "Yes," I answered. "I'm his daughter." It sounded strange to say out loud. Larry looked a little startled but smiled and winked at me. "She sure is," he said, and with that, we followed the nurse together.

Larry was indeed my father, and meeting him anchored me to the world in a way I'd never been before. There was no denying I was his daughter. It was as plain as the nose on our faces. Growing up, I never liked my nose; I'd always thought it was a little pug nose. Yet once I saw my father's face, I accepted mine. My nose was in my DNA and identified me with something beyond myself. Now I smiled every time I looked in the mirror.

Larry was also more like me in ways I'd never experienced with anyone else. We fit. We shared humor, tastes, habits, talents, and character traits. It was easy to be together, and I felt understood and loved in a way I can only describe as coming home to my true family. It was a powerful feeling.

When I glanced at Larry sitting on the exam table, one hand holding gauze over the injured other, I saw another likeness. His hands were like mine. I never liked my hands, especially my fingers, but when I saw my father's fingers, I understood they were the only fingers I could have, and they made sense. I accepted them, even welcomed them. My nose, my fingers—what if I had known why they looked like this all my life? Does it make it any easier when you are dissatisfied with some part of yourself to say, "Well, I got this from my family. I am one of them. I couldn't be different"? I grew up with no explanation for why I looked like I did, no genetic blueprint. If I wished parts of me were different, couldn't I make them so? If I dieted enough, couldn't I look like the model of the moment? But now I knew the stock I came from. No one in this family was six feet tall and reed thin, and I was one of them. It was a relief.

Our visit together flew by and left us eager for more. We planned for Larry to return with the rest of his family a month later and looked forward to our first complete Grogan family gathering on Nantucket.

That August, seven Grogans stepped off the plane. They began a week of first-time-to-Nantucket activities that included beach outings, exploring the cobblestoned streets of town, harborside dinners, and an awe-inspiring evening with the Boston Pops on Jetties Beach. In between excursions, we gathered around the pool and shared our individual experiences of my appearance in their lives. We repeated our stories endlessly, never interrupting each other, understanding that reliving the event was how we would each absorb and integrate the shock. We loved recounting the reactions of friends and strangers who heard our tale, and it was fun to be a narrator who elicited wide-eyed gasps.

We had an endless curiosity about one another. What were our childhoods like? Our homes, jobs, kids, and interests? We knew so little about each other yet felt so comfortable being together.

As we toured the island that week, I was happy introducing my new family to friends everywhere we went. At the Boston Pops concert on the beach, we were inundated with hoots and hugs as friends heard our story. And we loved the comments of strangers when, for example, we were waiting for a table at a restaurant and a random patron would survey our group, chuckle, and say, "Well, it's easy to see you're all related!"

I never tired of hearing that comment—one I'd never heard before in my life. It gave me goosebumps every time. The relation was particularly easy to see between Sean and me. We share the same smile and facial features. He is younger by ten years, but I tend to think of him as my big brother, perhaps because he is tall, strong, confident, and always caring for others. I feel safe and protected around him. While I saw the eyes and smile we shared, I didn't see similarities in our mannerisms. Nevertheless, they were very familiar, even if I couldn't quite place them. One day, as we stood in the kitchen, Sean leaned back to grab something off the counter behind him, and I realized, in that slight movement, it was exactly how my son, Will, moves. *Exactly*. I didn't know why I hadn't seen it sooner! Even more similarities came to light when Will and Sean were together. They both burned incense and candles daily, liked the same spicy foods, shared the same political views and sense of humor! Most important, they both had the most generous, caring hearts. It was wonderful to see them discover each other, and I wished Will could have known Sean as he was growing up, an uncle he could have related to and admired, as he did now.

On the Grogan family's final evening, I suggested watching a DVD of the Ric Burns film *Nantucket*, the one Larry saw at its premiere earlier in the summer. Everyone found a place in the living room, arms spread over the backs of sofas, feet propped up, and sweatshirts tossed aside. Moving to the back of the room, I ensured that everyone had a good view. I could practically recite the script line for line, yet the opening shots took my breath away every time. As the first long, dreaming notes played and the deep blue dawn appeared on-screen, I was incredibly proud to share the film with my new family. Everyone was silent as Ric Burns's magic filled the room, and they settled in as if this was something we'd done a thousand times before, a regular Sunday movie night with the family. Every cell in me was at peace, and I had the most profound sense of ease and belonging. Yet I couldn't have answered ten questions about anyone in that room.

Sharing Nantucket with the Grogans that first summer brought me great joy and deepened my sense of home on the island. Climbing into bed one night after their departure, I was surprised to see a brilliant white moon shimmering over the ocean and a dome of stars stretched over my head, over the house, folding everything up in a radiant cosmic snow globe. Resting my head on my pillow, I felt more at peace than I had in a long time. I was mesmerized by the dark curl of waves rolling through the light-scattered water. The words of one of my favorite childhood poems by Mildred Plew Meigs came to mind: "Zoon, zoon, cuddle, and croon, over the crinkling sea, the moon man flings him a silvered net fashioned of moonbeams three."* I was fully in the moment and so grateful for it. It felt wonderful. The light, the energy, the peace. I wanted to feel it forever.

---

* Mildred Plew Meigs, "Moon Song," lines 1–4.

CHAPTER EIGHTEEN

More Family Ties
2011

Larry talked a lot about my birth mother, Shirlie, while he was on Nantucket and even fantasized about the three of us getting together. This was completely unrealistic, but I was swept along into the fantasy and, at least, wanted to send her another letter. I wanted to tell her I'd spent time with Larry. I still wanted to know her and wanted her to know me. Silly of me. He was the man she'd never told, the man she'd recently hung up on. She wanted nothing to do with him.

After updating Gloria and the adoption agency on my wonderful summer visits, they urged me to send a second letter to Shirlie. Thinking back to my first letter, I wondered what I could say differently to appeal to her. What did she need to hear? What tone should I take? I crafted another letter, though it didn't sound like me; it was stiff and formal. I was deliberately trying something different. Softening the letter with photographs of Larry and me smiling together, I also included photos of my gardens, which looked like ones she'd posted online. If *I* didn't interest her, maybe my gardens would. I forwarded the letter to the agency, and they gladly sent it off.

Once more, I waited.

Once more, no response.

Case closed.

———

The holidays were in sight, the first Thanksgiving and Christmas since I'd met Larry, and I agonized over whether or not to tell my parents about him. My parents had encouraged me to search for my biological family when I was in college, working on my independent study, "Identity and Adoption"; however, I wasn't convinced they were sincere. Mom's voice was meek and subdued when we talked about it, and while I knew they would support me if I felt compelled to search, I understood it would hurt them. Now, unbeknownst to them, a search was complete, and I struggled with the truth. They were in their nineties, and I'd seen how much more they struggled with emotional stress. At their age, would they feel I was replacing them? Could they understand I had *expanded* my family, not reduced it?

My connection with my birth family didn't lessen my devotion to my parents. I spoke with them daily, handled their problems and concerns, managed their house, finances, and health care, and paid their bills. I'd always been the caretaker in my family, and meeting Larry didn't change that. Meeting him gave me a broader perspective on my life. As I pieced parts of me together, I brought a stronger self back to my parents, which allowed me to see with a more open and respectful heart, especially toward my mother. My heart softened. I had more patience. I saw her more objectively. She had many strengths, and though she could not show affection or be a devoted mother, she did not intend to hurt us. She did the best she could.

Another surprising consequence of meeting Larry was that now I could see myself as someone else's child, as Larry's daughter, and it was easier to imagine my adoptive parents' perspective. When they looked at me, did they wonder whose child I was, whose blood was in my veins? How often did *they* wonder who my birth parents were and how much I was like *them*? Did they grieve not having a little Audrey or Bob? I gained a more profound understanding of how generous my parents were to give me everything despite the fact that I *was* someone else's daughter. With that perspective my gratitude grew deeper.

There'd be enough loss in the coming years. I'd lose them to death. I didn't want to lose them before and wouldn't risk hurting them now. I wouldn't tell them about my pursuit. It really wasn't about them, anyway. This was about me and my loss, my search, my blood, and my healing.

I did fantasize about both my families sitting together around the Thanksgiving table. The family who made me and the family who raised me. I imagined them all smiling and sharing stories, and this image brought me relief, though I didn't understand why that felt so important. It didn't seem unusual to wish for this Hollywood holiday vision—imagining everybody happy, united, and accepting of one another. In those early stages of reunion, I didn't realize how confused I was regarding both families in my life. Two families, yet not a full-fledged member of either. My biology separated me from my adopted family, yet my lack of common experiences with my biological family did the same. I'd always wondered, *Who am I?* and though now I had a lot more information, there were new pieces of a puzzle. Integrating the biological and adopted me would be a long and solitary journey.

I did tell my adopted siblings about Larry. My older brother, Eric, and his wife, Gail, were very supportive, and I wondered if Eric might want to do his own search, but it wasn't feasible in the wake of his debilitating stroke.

My younger sister, Susie, was inspired by my search and applied to the agency. I went with her for her interview. We were shocked to learn the agency already had a letter in their files from her birth mother, Ellen, written decades ago in hopes of meeting her daughter before moving to England. For reasons unknown, the agency put the letter in my sister's file without contacting her, even though they already had a letter from Susie saying she wanted to be contacted if her birth mother ever inquired. And now the agency couldn't help facilitate a reunion since they didn't have resources for an international search. Susie was crushed but wrote down her mother's name and last known address without knowing what the next steps might be.

Heartbroken for my sister and her birth mother, Rick and I hired a private investigator in London to search for Ellen. We'd receive periodic updates from the investigator, at first all discouraging. He found Ellen's original British address but discovered she'd moved away, and none of her old neighbors seemed to know where she went. After scouring British resources, the investigator was certain she was no longer in England but had no clue where in the world she might be. We asked him to search further and were told there were twelve women in the world with her same name, and it might take significant effort and expense to discover which was Susie's mother. He offered suggestions for a possible path forward, and we asked him to proceed.

A few weeks later, my phone rang while I was running errands on a very ordinary November day. I was driving, so I hesitated to answer, but when I saw the call was coming from an international number, I hit Accept.

It was the investigator to say he'd found Ellen in France, but I was skeptical, knowing how many Ellens he had to check out. My hand slipped lazily around the steering wheel as I turned through a bend and asked why he was sure this was the right woman.

"Well, let me read her Twitter post from October fourth." The investigator paused and cleared his throat. "Happy Fiftieth Birthday to my darling red-haired daughter, wherever you may be in this world, know I have always loved you."

Shivers shot through me from head to toe, and I worked to keep the car steady on the road. Oh my God, he'd found her!

Pulling to the side of the road, I wrote down the international phone number the investigator gave me and called it immediately. The voicemail greeting was in French, and I wasn't sure I was leaving a message for the right person, but left details and my return number. I didn't want to call Susie until I knew this was indeed the correct Ellen, but I did call Gloria at the adoption agency to give her the information. Gloria called me back a few hours later to say she had spoken with Ellen, who was indeed Susie's mother, and let me know she'd connected Ellen and Susie. When I spoke with Ellen, she'd already talked to Susie and was weeping with joy.

Ellen came to visit six weeks later, and she and Susie stayed with us in New Jersey. It was wonderful to hear her life story and watch her reunite with her one and only child. Ellen was in college when she got pregnant, and she and Susie's father, who were in love, eloped, running to the new parish of an old family priest. Instead of marrying them, the priest called their parents. Ellen was then locked in her parents' home for the duration of her pregnancy and pressured to give the baby up for adoption. She remembered holding and loving Susie before she had to surrender her and never had any other children.

It was amazing to see how much Susie and Ellen were alike; they loved the same foods and colors, shared the same interests, and had the same impulses. Their resemblance was uncanny, and even though I'd experienced the same when I met Larry, watching it happen to someone else was incredible and validating.

Susie was fortunate to hear Ellen's stories about wanting to keep her, reaching out to the adoption agency to try and meet her, and how much she'd thought of and loved her all these years—things I'd hoped for in my search.

Ellen also brought photographs and information about Susie's birth father, who'd died by suicide in his forties. This was both affirming and disturbing for Susie, who suffered from depression and suicidal thoughts throughout her life. She empathized with his pain and grieved that she would never know him. She reached out to her half siblings on her father's side, who not only lived nearby but knew their father had given a baby daughter up for adoption. When they answered Susie's phone call, they told her they'd been waiting for this call all their lives. Susie bonded immediately with her half sister, Nicole, and was proud to introduce her grown children to their new aunt. They all described the same feelings I'd had when I met my biological family—recognition, affirmation, acceptance, and belonging.

CHAPTER NINETEEN

Borrowed Time

2013

Two years after I met Larry, something wasn't right. He wasn't responding to emails as quickly, and his replies were often confusing. When I saw him, he was oddly flat, with slow reactions, and he had lost weight.

Just before their family visit to Nantucket that summer, Gayle found Larry on the floor of his home and rushed him to the hospital. After two weeks of testing, the results were inconclusive. The only recommendation was for Larry to eat regular meals and drink plenty of fluids to ward off the side effects of his heart medicine. The family was scheduled to come to Nantucket just a few days after his release from the hospital, and determined to join the group, Larry got on the plane with Gayle and Sean's assistance.

When Rick and I met them at the airport, I was shocked by Larry's appearance. Unshaven and dressed more casually than usual, he was frail, much more so than at our visit two months earlier. But excited to be together, we rushed to load luggage into our SUVs and headed home along Milestone Road. With bright blue skies overhead, cyclists and joggers sailed along the bike path as we laughed and chatted, looking forward to the coming week.

Once home, Rick and I sorted suitcases. Larry would be in the guest house, along with my half sister, Jessica, and her one-year-old baby, Regan. Rick grabbed bags and walked them to their accommodations, where he suggested Larry wait in the living room while he helped Jess and the baby upstairs. Unfortunately, Larry didn't wait and started up the stairs after them, falling backward and hitting hard on the landing.

We called an ambulance, and when it pulled away, Sean, Gayle, and I raced to meet it at Nantucket Cottage Hospital. We found Larry in a small examining room, swathed in white sheets and blankets. Though he was alert and talking, he was shaking. Even warm blankets didn't help. None of us realized how much pain he was in and were alarmed when the doctor told us his arm sustained a severe puncture break, and they needed to medevac him to Mass General in Boston. The challenges of off-island medical care were suddenly upon me, starting with who would go to Boston, how they would get there, and where they would stay. While I assured Sean and Gayle this was routine for Nantucket, I was dealing with emergency medical decisions for people I barely knew. Had I grown up with this family, I'd have a better instinct for answering every question.

Soon the MedFlight helicopter pilots strode in, strapped Larry onto their gurney, and rushed him out to the helipad. Running to the parking lot, we watched the helicopter whir its long, silver blades faster and faster and lift into the sky, tilting for a moment before it pulled away like a giant dragonfly. Sean and Gayle decided to go to Boston, while their sons stayed with Rick and me. The next plane to Boston was leaving in minutes, so we raced to the airport, where they ran across the tarmac with nothing but the clothes on their backs, poor Gayle in shorts and a tank top.

Larry was in Mass General for the next few days, and in addition to setting his broken arm, doctors ordered a broad range of tests. Later that week, Sean and Gayle returned to Nantucket with Larry in a wheelchair, a cast on his arm and a bandage on his head, looking tired and pale. Over the next few days, I was impressed by how Sean and Gayle's teenage sons stepped up to help Larry with even his most personal needs. It must have been a shock to see their grandfather so disabled, but they pitched right in. We all settled into a new routine sitting with Larry on the back porch where he often held baby Regan and sang "Hambone" to her. Regan watched him with wide eyes and a sweet smile, and I noticed something about the shape of her face that reminded me of my baby pictures—how amazing to see the Grogan DNA in yet another generation!

There was a level of concern from Larry's children that seemed out of proportion to the situation. Was I missing something? Or was I just not familiar with how this family responded to crises?

At the end of that unsettling week, everyone gathered by the pool for a lobster dinner. While we'd lost much of our vacation, sitting around the table that night was comforting, and I felt embraced as we sat together. The warm summer evening grew dark and still; candles cast amber light on contented faces. Cigars were lit, and the pool glowed like a gem in the deep shadows. Gayle wheeled Larry back to the guest house and put him to bed, giving the remaining siblings and spouses a moment to exhale. We leaned back and looked at one another with a can-you-believe-this-week expression, and that's when Sean told me.

He said he'd been waiting for Rick to return from his work week so I had support before receiving the news. Larry's tests revealed he was riddled with cancer, which was well advanced, and he had only a short time to live.

I looked at Sean blankly for a moment as tears filled my eyes. "No," I sobbed. "No! We just found each other!"

I remember Rick's arm around my shoulder, the orange candle glow, and Sean's sad eyes across the table. It was hard to breathe, and somewhere, deep in my core, the wound was ripping open again.

———————

Two years after we met, thirty-two days after receiving his prognosis, Larry passed away. Yes, we had time to say goodbye during those thirty-two days, but we had barely said hello. Two years isn't enough time to build a store of memories, but each one I have is precious, and my father's hands holding mine are both my first memory of him and my last.

The first time we met, that snowy January day, he stood in front of me, his hands lying over mine. He looked right into my face and said, "You're Janet." I can still feel the warmth of those hands and the gentle strength of his fingers. A sense of completion flowed between us and bonded us forever.

On what would be our last day together, he lay on his sofa, as he had for days, and pushed up on the pillows to talk. We said everything you would want to at such a time, how much it meant to find each other, and what joy it was to be together. Still enamored with each other, we'd not had time for disappointments or resentments. We'd been saying these things to each other since we met, trying to make up for a lost past, but now we were saying them to each other as we lost our future. When I bent over to kiss him goodbye that final day, he grabbed my hands, and I was amazed by his strength. He held my hands so tightly they vibrated with everything that couldn't be put into words, the depth of his feelings and our connection. They said he didn't want to leave me but knew he would and understood how difficult his passing would be for me. They offered comfort and peace and gave me an absolutely tangible memory of love. I can still feel them. I will always feel them.

People said, "Just be glad you had two years together."

I smiled, knowing the comment was meant to comfort me, but I was heartbroken. Whenever I thought of Larry, I'd catch my breath and stifle a cry. My eyes welled up, my throat tightened, and a familiar pain opened in my gut. I wanted to sob, and wished someone would put their arms around me and weep, "Oh, to have just found him and then lost him so soon, I can't imagine!" I wanted them to know my pain and tell me they understood. I was bereft. I was a child sobbing for the loss of everything I had ever known. I felt like my core had disappeared again, and no other attachments in my life could secure me. I wanted to howl. I wanted him back. I needed more time.

Larry and I talked about writing our story, and I thought there'd be plenty of years to do so. He loved to read and had won a prize for writing in college, and I loved the idea of telling this story from both perspectives. I wanted his voice to explain what it was like, at age seventy-five, to learn he'd fathered a child fifty-six years ago. What did it take to absorb me into his life? I know I stirred up regrets, longings, and many "what ifs" that came with the memories of being a young man and the pretty girl he was crazy about.

Would there have been greater resistance if we'd met when we were younger? Would we have connected if I'd come to Larry when he was married, raising a family, or consumed with work? How capricious is love? Is it all about timing?

I was fortunate that Larry's family welcomed me into the clan. They could have seen me as a disrupter, an outlier to be viewed with suspicion or scorn, but I never felt anything other than acceptance and love. Sean once heard me use the term "half sister" and told me he didn't like that term. "You're my sister, period," he said. "I don't think of you as anything else."

Most people in Larry's wider circle of friends and colleagues didn't know I existed, and when it came to the funeral, I expected to sit quietly in the back. My siblings insisted I stand on the receiving line with them and do a reading at the service. "You're his daughter. You stand with us." Their candor surprised me as we stood in line to greet guests, and with each curious hand extended toward me, one of my siblings would introduce me: "This is Larry's daughter, Janet."

Mourners came from every facet of Larry's life. Many were old school friends. We wondered what these classmates would think if they knew who my mother was—one of their own, Miss Middletown High School herself. Toward the end of one visitation, an attractive couple stepped forward and reached out to shake my hand and extend their sympathy. They introduced themselves as schoolmates of Larry's, and Sean introduced me as Larry's daughter. Standing behind the receiving line, Rick abruptly stepped through and addressed them. "You might remember Janet's mother, Shirlie Jones," he said boldly. The couple looked at me and gasped, stepping back. "Oh my gosh, you do look like her!" the woman whispered. As they grabbed each other's arms and rushed off, I froze. Had Rick just outed Shirlie at Larry's funeral? Wasn't this terribly inappropriate? I heard Sean laughing and looked over, shocked.

"I think that's great," Sean said. "Rick is looking out for you. He is taking care of you, defending your interests. Good for him!"

Rick was tired of Shirlie dismissing me. He often remarked that she wasn't entitled to deny my heritage, and since she wasn't stepping up, he took an opportunity to declare a connection between my birth mother and me. I wasn't just Larry's daughter. I was Shirlie's too. I stood with Larry's family at his funeral in her hometown, shaking hands with their old school friends while she still wanted to disclaim my existence. With Larry gone, Rick felt compelled to do something to dispel the secret. He knew I still hoped that Shirlie contained some vestige of compassion and we would meet someday.

Larry spent his career as a New York State Trooper, and Sean was well along into his own career as a Trooper. In tribute to their service, State Police Honor Guards stood over Larry's casket at the funeral home, and on the day of the service, a police motorcade assembled to escort the cortege to the cemetery. As the long procession wound its way to the church, officers halted traffic at every intersection and held their arms in salute until we passed. Tears rolled down my cheeks as I watched each gloved hand rise and the streets stop in Larry's honor.

Returning to Nantucket after the funeral, thick grief smothered me for days. I slept deeply and dreamlessly but woke up crying. I bumped through the house in a daze. Then a stretch of relief would come, and I'd try to do something normal like go to the grocery store but would fall apart there, cry all the way home, and crawl back into bed again.

I had an insatiable need to look at the ocean and sky, and when I thought of leaving, I couldn't breathe. I looked to the waves to flow into me and deliver some comfort, some peace, some deep, primal healing. I needed to watch the light, the colors, the sky over the sea, and feel the energy renew me—the fresh, salty, wet energy that rolls off the sea. I wanted to watch the waves break again and again, to crest and curl and crash, see the green water pull away and the white foam scatter in silence until the next wave exploded down with thunder. I didn't want to do anything, think about anything, or be anywhere else. I just wanted to look out over the sea, endlessly, mindlessly, trying to numb my grief that Larry was gone too soon, and I was untethered once more.

CHAPTER TWENTY

Mourning Calls Again
2013–2014

Three years had passed since the agency first contacted Shirlie and she'd refused to meet me. Larry's recent death made me yearn for her again, despite his anecdotes about her dismissive behavior at high school reunions or how she'd hung up on him when he'd called to confirm my existence. Why was I driven to meet the woman who'd repeatedly rejected me?

Because she was my mother. I was part of her and had an instinct, a cellular drive, to reconnect with her before I could feel whole.

With mixed emotions, I wrote another letter to her. Anger drove me this time, and I wrote from the heart, using my authentic voice, not a polite or cultivated one. While I still acknowledged her point of view, I pressed mine. My letter read, in part:

The reality of me—the fact that I was created and born and adopted— is not just something that happened to you and caused you embarrass- ment and pain. It happened to me. You seem to have discarded me and moved on, as quickly as possible, back to a life where you didn't have to think about me. However, being adopted defined my life, and I never, for one day, did not wonder where I came from and who I really was.

You don't get to pretend that I don't exist. You created me, I am your daughter, and I do exist, and if you had one ounce of empathy, you would be more interested in meeting me than worrying about your reputation over something that happened fifty-nine years ago.

I am not showing up at your door expecting anything more than the desire to make a connection. And doesn't that scenario also offer you the best opportunity to make peace with this part of your life?

This should be an opportunity that helps us integrate a loss we both experienced when I was put up for adoption. I am awestruck at the depth of denial you must live with. Everyone who knows this story tells me it is your loss that we aren't meeting. But I know it remains both of our losses, and for that, I am deeply sad.

I didn't go through the agency. I knew who she was and where she worked, so I sent it directly to her office, Private and Confidential. Friends asked what I expected this time. I said I was telling her off to be done with her, but that wasn't the truth. Her rejection hurt me so much I didn't know what else to do. I was poking the bear for any reaction and hoping for a miracle.

Yet once again, there was no response at all.

A few months after I sent the letter, I had lunch with Gloria, the social worker who'd located Shirlie three years earlier. Gloria was disappointed there'd been no reunion with Shirlie. "You should write to her children, your five siblings. You are all adults. They have the right to make up their own minds about knowing you. Shirlie doesn't have the right to make that decision for them."

I pushed my plate away. "No, I don't want to 'out' her to her kids. That's her worst fear. How would that help?"

"It could help *you*. Through them, there would be a connection to your mother and that side of the family."

No, I didn't want to contact Shirlie's children, my siblings. I was afraid Shirlie would be so angry she'd never speak to me (however likely that already was), and I imagined her children would close ranks to protect her from a pushy stranger. (Stranger? I was their sister!) No, I didn't want to blow that family up. I didn't want anyone to be mad at me.

Oh my God: *I didn't want anyone to be mad at me?* I didn't want them to be mad at me because I still hoped she would love me. It was pathetic.

Gloria lifted the napkin from her lap and set it on the table. "I hope you'll consider this further."

As she stood to leave, she handed me some papers. "These are the names of adoption support groups in your area. You might want to reach out to one."

She smiled patiently, and I knew she had experience and perspective I should listen to. She had guided me well, and I trusted her. However, I didn't contact any support groups or consider contacting my siblings. I was exhausted. I needed a break. I didn't do anything in the misguided hope of distancing myself from the emotional toll this journey was taking.

A year later, my brother Eric was suffering tremendous pain. Most of his body was paralyzed from the stroke he'd suffered four years earlier, but spending every day in a wheelchair had damaged his spine. Medication brought no relief and fogged his brain, so he decided to undergo spinal surgery. The surgeon believed his body could handle the eight-hour procedure.

I drove to Pennsylvania to be with Gail on a cold but sunny November day, and we both secretly wondered if Eric would survive.

We understood this was his choice. His life had become too limited to live in pain, and we prepared to accept any outcome. But as our wait exceeded ten hours, my anxiety knotted every muscle into a dull, throbbing ache. By evening we were the only ones left in the waiting room, and folded into our chairs, we took shallow breaths, and let out long, exhausted exhales. When the surgeon finally appeared, he reported that everything went well, except for a "minor cardiac event," which they managed. Gail broke down with relief and sobbed into her hands. I was surprised Eric had made it through.

After a few days in the ICU, Eric was cleared to begin in-patient physical therapy. True to form, he worked hard at it. Gail spent every waking hour with him, just as she did after his stroke, and at the end of a grueling week, she drove home exhausted but hopeful.

But then our phone rang too early the next morning. It was Gail, gasping, choking on her words, telling me the morning nurse found Eric unresponsive. He was on life support. Rick and I rushed to the hospital, as did my younger brother, Mark. We embraced one another, hearts pressed together, arms holding tight, heads bowed as the nurses pulled extra chairs around Eric's bed. The ventilator pumped, and Eric looked peaceful as his chest rose and fell with the rhythm. We jumped at any movement of his fingers or flutter of his eyes, only to have a nurse explain our hopes away. Four of us sat in Eric's hospital room, considering options, and Rick commented it felt strange to be making life-and-death decisions without any "adult supervision." Where were the grown-ups? We were all middle-aged adults shocked and overwhelmed by what we were facing.

We talked about Mom and Dad, who lived over an hour away, and wondered if we should go get them. Would they make it here before Eric passed? Would they have time to say goodbye? Would they be able to handle this? The death of a child is said to be the most stressful event anyone can face, and they were ninety-two and ninety-three. But they deserved the opportunity to say goodbye to their son, and Rick and I volunteered to get them.

Before we left, I had a moment alone with Eric. I told him I loved him, thanked him for always protecting me, and promised to be there for Gail. I floated to the car in shock. I couldn't believe I'd just said goodbye to my brother and prayed we'd get Mom and Dad back in time. We drove as fast as we could through the black night, yellow lines flying back into our eyes. I leaned forward, focusing ahead as if my will could pull us directly to their house, though I dreaded having to deliver this news to my parents.

Mom and Dad weren't home when we got there, a twist I hadn't expected. I paced the living room wondering where they were. My reflection stood in the dark picture window, with my coat still on, and my brow furrowed. I looked old.

Before my parents returned, I received the call from Gail that Eric had passed. Rick and I sat down and wrapped our arms around each other. My eyes teared, but I didn't cry because all I could think about was how I'd tell my parents Eric had died. The last they'd heard, he had come through the surgery and was recovering well.

Eventually, car doors slammed outside and Mom and Dad inched their way up the front walk with their good friends, the Eveleths, who'd taken them out to dinner. They were surprised but happy to see Rick and me standing at their front door, but as Mom and Dad shuffled past me, their friends paused and looked up with questioning eyes. When I shook my head and cast my eyes down, they understood and made an excuse to leave. Dad went to the kitchen to put their leftovers away while Mom shrugged her coat off and said something about a cup of tea. Rick asked them to come sit in the living room instead.

I stood in the redbrick house where I grew up and spoke to my parents as slowly and gently as possible, though I was in shock and didn't hear my own words. A bright light stabbed me in the eyes, and my feet wavered on the thick, dusty carpet. There were photographs everywhere—on the piano, on the walls—and next to my father's chair was a large black-and-white picture of Eric, age two, holding me, age six months. Now my mother sat weeping, and my father was silent and still. They would hardly be able to speak of this again. It was too much for them to bear.

For years after Eric's death, I felt his presence frequently, and it always surprised me to sense him standing off to the side as intensely as I did. I felt closer to him in death than we had been in life and didn't understand why he remained with me for so long. I didn't experience the same thing with other loved ones. The early death of a sibling is complicated and brings death uncomfortably close. Maybe I just couldn't accept it, or maybe I was trying to protect the integrity of my adopted family. Eric was the first of us to pass away, but my adopted parents were close to the end of their lives. It felt as if my borrowed family was about to disintegrate, and with Larry's death a year earlier, and Shirlie's continued denial, it was too much loss and abandonment. Maybe I "kept Eric around" because I couldn't integrate any further grief. Or maybe he stayed around to help me through one more time.

CHAPTER TWENTY-ONE

Wait . . . Hold the Phone!

2016

Six years after I initiated a search for my birth mother, three years after I last tried to contact her, I got mad. Again. I became agitated reading *Blue Nights* by Joan Didion, in which she writes about her adopted daughter's life and death. In one passage, Didion describes the extreme measures she took to prevent her daughter's birth mother from finding them. In others she wrote candidly about her insecurity as an adopted parent. Both irked me, though I did appreciate Didion's hindsight when she wrote, "I believed as I did so that I was protecting both Quintana and her mother. I tell you this now by way of suggesting the muddled impulses that can go hand in hand with adoption."

Didion was pleased when a young Quintana told her she didn't want to search for her biological mother. I said the same thing when I was young, but it wasn't true—I didn't want to hurt my adoptive mother. Did Quintana know that Didion had her birth mother's full name and location? Had my adoptive mother known my birth mother's name and location, I would have wanted to know, even expected it to be my right as an adult. I'd have considered it a tremendous betrayal if she had it and withheld it from me. Maybe Quintana never wanted to search, but deciding whether or not to do so is complicated. Adoptive parents unwittingly communicate their insecurities to their children, and the fear of hurting their loving adoptive parents negates free choice in any adoptee's decision to search.

When Quintana was an adult, and her full biological sister found her, Didion wrote "On the other hand, I told myself, it now seemed too late, not the right time. There comes a point, I told myself, at which a family is, for better or for worse, finished." Didion wanted to believe there was an expiration date for the com-plications of adoption, an end point at which her daughter would be safely hers and not threatened by deeper issues of identity and origin.

A family is never finished for an adoptee who doesn't know who they are or where they came from. There is no end point to the feel-ings of abandonment and loss, especially when those feelings aren't identified and dealt with. Didion's previous books were noted for her astute observations and research into social and political issues, and I was surprised how little she understood about her adoptive child's needs and how best to support them. Then again, in the years she raised her daughter, there was little written on the subject, and no one thought much about it.

After reading *Blue Nights*, I wanted to reread *The Primal Wound*—a book that brilliantly details the adoptee's experience. It is so accurate, it makes my stomach fall and floods me with anxiety, but I turned to it again. As expected, revisiting it opened up that deep, dark hole in my middle, but gripping the pages like a lifeline, I read past the most triggering pages, and toward the end of the book, these sentences spoke to me:

> If the adoptee has done everything in his power to get this birth-
> mother to acknowledge him and relate to him in some way, he
> may want to contact his siblings instead. This is his right, whether

the birth mother wants it or not. He did not ask to be cut off from his genealogy, and he can't be expected to accept it. If the siblings are adults, it is up to them to decide whether or not they want to establish relationships with him. The mother can't make that decision for them. These relationships, although not as powerful as that with the mother, can be very healing. And sometimes the rest of her children can convince the birth mother to change her mind about relating to the child she relinquished.

This was just what Gloria had told me years before! I hadn't had the guts then, but I was ready now. I had nothing to lose. There was no relationship with my birth mother and none to hope for. If all I did was make Shirlie mad, then so be it. I was mad. She could be too.

It happened quickly. I wrote the letter on Wednesday, one draft. I had the names of my siblings from the high school reunion pages Larry shared with me, so I searched online for their addresses and prepared the envelopes. Since they all lived close to my home in New Jersey, I sent the letters Overnight Delivery so that they would receive them simultaneously.

Now there was no turning back. I had launched my own shock and awe campaign. I hoped at least one of the five siblings would reach out to me, but I didn't expect it. After all, they'd been raised by Shirlie and might be just like her and not care. I told myself they all had full and busy lives with little room for an interloper.

The following afternoon, unexpected exhaustion overcame me. I couldn't stay awake. Me, the insomniac who had trouble sleeping. I lay down on the family room sofa and fell into a deep sleep. When my cell phone rang at 7:00 p.m., I fumbled to answer. "Hello?"

"Hello, Janet? This is your sister, Dyanne." Dyanne's voice was low and warm, and she seemed as surprised to hear my voice as I was to hear hers.

Dyanne told me she wept reading my letter, and while our mother was cold and self-centered, she was devastated to see her be this unfeeling. She admitted Shirlie had not been a good mother, commented I was lucky not to have been raised by her, and said she'd spoken with our sister, Carol, who was also appalled by Shirlie's behavior and anxious to talk with me. I know we said more, but I can't remember what. I was in shock, and the details didn't stick. My brain struggled to keep up with the experience. I was flabbergasted that a sibling had reached out to me so quickly and warmly.

When Rick arrived home from work, I was sitting at the kitchen island on the phone with Dyanne, and he hovered nearby, waiting for details. After I hung up with Dyanne, I gave him a breathless synopsis before calling my other new sister, Carol. When she answered, we whispered our first tentative hellos.

Carol was shaken by our mother's denial of me. She didn't have a good relationship with Shirlie and hadn't spoken to her in seven years, but she said she could never have imagined this and was shocked at how cruel Shirlie was.

The eldest in her family, Carol was born eighteen months after me. She was the first child born to Shirlie and William Chalmers, the man Shirlie married within a year of my birth. Carol told me she remembered her mother, *our* mother, telling her never to have children because they ruined your life, which was confusing because Shirlie went on to have four more babies. When Carol was seventeen, Shirlie kicked her out of the house, and she went to live with our grandmother, Grams. She remembered asking Grams why Shirlie had five children if she didn't want them, and Grams replied, "There's even one more," without further explanation.

We talked for quite a while. The conversation felt easy and relaxed, like family members sharing stories, like sisters catching up. After Carol and I hung up, texts began to fly between Dyanne, Carol, and me with photos, anecdotes, and continued awe. Rick was anxious to hear the details, but it was difficult for my swirling brain to detach from the texts and fill him in. He finally kissed me and said, "Focus on your sisters. You can tell me about it tomorrow. I'm heading to bed."

We three sisters finally said goodnight and stopped texting. I wasn't ready to sleep, nor was Dyanne, who sent an email saying she and our brother, Steven, were going to Shirlie's in the morning to confront her. She said she was rereading my letter with tears streaming down her face.

The mention of Steven was a surprise because Carol and Dyanne said they didn't expect their brothers to get involved. They explained the boys had always been closer to Shirlie, who'd let them "run wild." I asked Dyanne what Steven's reaction was to my letter, and she said he'd been as shocked as she had been, which surprised her because she'd never known him to be critical of their mother.

It was very late, but I remained at the kitchen island in a daze. I'll admit there was some comfort in hearing that Shirlie was cold and uncaring, and I wasn't the only one to whom she was hard and heartless.

I climbed upstairs to bed, but while my exhausted body lay motionless, my brain couldn't shut down. Had this really happened? I tried to play it all back but couldn't retrieve the details, and finally, blessedly, I fell asleep.

At eight the following morning the phone rang. It was my new brother Steven. Touched by his call, I said I was sorry for the pain and upset this might cause the family, but he assured me I'd done the right thing, and his empathy was palpable. He was heading to Shirlie's and said it wouldn't be easy, but he'd let me know how it went. I imagined the roof blowing off Shirlie's house when they confronted her. She'd be furious with me. Who the hell did I think I was? Who was this troublemaker who'd hunted her down and was now exposing her secret?

Your daughter, Shirlie. I'm your daughter.

Later that day, emails from Dyanne reported that upon hearing I'd sent a letter to my siblings, Shirlie scoffed and said it sounded like "something your sister would do," referring to Carol, who'd sent Shirlie several "poison pen" letters during the years they didn't speak.

Dyanne replied, "My *sister* did do this!"

Steven and Dyanne told Shirlie they couldn't believe she'd been so cruel; they expected her to make it right and meet me, and they'd be disappointed if she didn't. When she said she needed more time, they told her she'd already had plenty. Dyanne speculated that Shirlie would try to put it out of her mind and bury it again, but they would keep on her and hope.

With every new email or text, every plot turn, Rick and I felt as if we'd landed inside a movie, watching a story unfold around us.

In an attempt to wrangle the information and emotions of the previous twenty-four hours, I emailed the friends and family who'd supported me during my search. The email was long and rambling, loaded with more details than anyone probably cared to read, but writing it out helped me sort through it. Within hours, friends sent emails congratulating me on contacting my siblings and suggesting celebrations—but I felt far from celebratory. I was exhausted and confused. I'd hoped to meet a mother like me, someone I could see myself in and feel a connection with. There would be no joy or "coming home" with Shirlie. She would not help heal my primal wound. She was, in fact, making it worse.

I made slow, aimless circles throughout the house. I didn't want to talk about it, but I didn't know what to do with myself. How was I supposed to process this? There was so much to take in, so many siblings, so much about Shirlie—and nothing about her was good. She sounded awful. I had a horrible mother.

Somehow I made it through the weekend, reeling from everything I'd heard, and by Monday, the conversations were receding, and I felt more like myself. Every once in a while, I'd stop and wonder if this had really happened and question what had been said in those conversations. It began to feel like a dream I couldn't recall.

When I finally settled back at my desk and opened my email, all seemed routine, and it was a relief.

At 2:01 p.m., there was a ping on my iPhone, and a text popped up.

"Janet, If I call you, are you available to talk? Shirlie"

I swear my heart stopped. I stared down at the message.

Had I really just been contacted by my birth mother?

And did she really want to talk?

It was too soon. I wasn't prepared! Should I respond? I was terrified. I needed a witness to this moment, someone to know I was about to jump off the ledge into the unknown. But I was home alone. There would be no witness, no hand to hold, no safety net for this leap.

My reply: "Yes, of course."

As soon as I hit Send, the blood drained from my head, and the room tilted. I moved into the living room to sit down. I remember the sky outside was remarkably blue and the grass a bright April green. I took a deep breath and braced myself for the call to come through.

I don't remember how we greeted each other, but I said I was surprised to receive the call, and Shirlie replied that she hadn't been happy to find out I had written to her children.

"Yes, I appreciate that. I am sorry I had to be the one to tell them."

Silence.

Starting again, I launched into why I'd always wanted to meet her and brought up some things I'd learned we had in common— gardens, photography, and clothes. She responded, and we began a conversation, but my mind was distracted by the reality that the woman I was talking to, this unfamiliar voice on the phone, was my mother! *My mother!* The woman who'd denied me so many times! The woman I wondered about every day of my life! Shouldn't the world stop for a moment? Shouldn't trumpets sound? Where was a witness? I needed a witness! My mind traced through the halls and rooms of the house, like liquid into every nook and cranny, to confirm that I was the singular soul in residence. Then I focused on the conversation as if my life depended on it. I needed answers to sixty-one years of questions, and this might be my only chance.

It had to be light, friendly, and nonthreatening. Direct questions about my birth and adoption were not to be asked. I knew that much. We traversed thin ice. A step too hard would plunge us into deep waters, maybe forever. I wanted her to know me, like me, and miss me. I wanted her to want me.

We talked about our favorite flowers (peonies, lilacs, roses) and how we liked to photograph them (close up), but I didn't reveal I'd seen her photographs on her Realtor website or how similar they were to mine. We talked about clothes and shopping, both of us admitting to excesses. We shared the joy of collecting, especially porcelain and items of Asian design, and how we loved being surrounded by objects that made our hearts sing. The conversation began to flow, so I leaned back into the sofa cushions and put my feet up. Across the room, the polished black piano gleamed, and birch trees rustled in sun and shadows outside the window.

I touched on the subject of adoption, sometimes talking about myself and other times referring to my adopted siblings. Shirlie seemed surprised that I longed to see someone I looked like. "Didn't the agency match you with your adoptive parents?"

Her nineteen-year-old mind must have believed there would be a precise physical match. I explained it was more regional—Northern European in general, not specific to nationality or individual features. When I spoke about siblings not being well-matched in temperament and personality, she asked, "How did you fit with your family?" She seemed genuinely concerned. "I fit in very well," I told her, and she sounded relieved. Of course, I didn't tell her I fit in well because I was scared and anxious, desperate for love and security.

Her questions about physical and temperamental matches annoyed me. They reminded me how unrealistic the adoption process was, how sugarcoated the promises were—hand the baby off and everything will be fine; a baby doesn't know anything; a baby can't tell a substitute mother from its biological mother; a baby doesn't remember the feeling of abandonment. They also reminded me how young Shirlie was and how easy it was for her to believe anything.

Before the call ended, Shirlie told me she hadn't been trying to forget *me*, just an awful experience. She said I sounded like a lovely person, and she looked forward to meeting me. She hoped she could help provide some of the missing pieces I sought.

I was stunned. I hadn't expected that much from her, especially after the conversations with my siblings, who described a cold, selfish, and uncaring woman. Although they also told me how charming and friendly Shirlie was in social situations and warned me that she lied easily, none of that came to mind during our conversation. Nor did it occur to me that I was being manipulated—that Shirlie was placating her grown children, pretending to do the right thing, telling me what I wanted to hear with no intention of ever following through. Such behavior was unthinkable to me. I took her at her word and hoped to forge a relationship with this woman, my long-lost mother.

When we hung up, the room was still. The light had grayed. I was suddenly aware of how large and empty the house felt. I stood slowly, steadying myself before searching the house, in vain, for a witness. Maybe someone had come home. Maybe someone was there to assure me that yes, this had happened, I spoke with my mother. Yes, she was real. I clutched my phone, stared at the empty black screen, and wished some evidence of the call remained. I wished I could play it back.

My God, I had finally talked to my mother. After sixty-one years.

CHAPTER TWENTY-TWO

New Sisters

2016

In the days that followed, friends reached out to me, but I couldn't put my reactions into words. Much of what I was feeling defied language and I mostly just needed to be alone to digest this from the inside out. I had to accept all this new information, allow it alongside everything I knew about myself, then let it settle in some unseen part of me so I could get used to it being there.

Since I'd sent the letter to my siblings, everything about my life had changed, yet nothing was different. I was in a state of suspended animation, eager to meet my new family, but no one suggested we get together. No one was calling. I felt like a silly girl sitting beside the phone, waiting for a date. Every day I wondered, Will someone call today? Maybe they didn't really want to meet me; there was no rush to bring me into their lives. Conversations rolled around in my head, and I was exhausted and weepy.

Finally, Rick suggested I invite my new sisters and their husbands to dinner the following weekend. They're the ones I'd spoken with the most and felt closest to. Although I'd talked to one of my brothers, Steven, and liked him very much, I hadn't spoken with my other brothers and was aware that Carol was estranged from all three brothers. Dyanne had confirmed that Shirlie wasn't ready for further contact, despite her comments on our phone call, nor could I imagine a dinner where Shirlie had to confront me along with Carol, the daughter she hadn't spoken to for seven years! This first dinner would be for sisters and husbands only.

I had been afraid to rush them, or insert myself, but I couldn't wait another minute. Sending a text inviting them to join us at our favorite restaurant, I was relieved to receive their replies within minutes—they'd love to.

All day Saturday, I worried I wouldn't look like them. What if I was more like my father's family, and this family didn't recognize our connection? I wanted them to see me and know that I belonged to them. I wanted to feel like I was coming home.

I worried about what to wear and settled on a silk blouse and a cashmere sweater in my favorite turquoise color. The tactile feel of both fabrics was critical. I didn't think of the physical sensations of my clothes when I went to meet Larry, but they seemed important to me that evening. My skin wanted to feel the comfort. I wanted to feel enveloped. As we drove to the restaurant, I wondered how we'd recognize each other. We'd exchanged some photos, flattering ones from me, and I was worried they wouldn't recognize the everyday me.

Rick and I checked in with the maître d'. We were the first to arrive, and I was unsure how and where to wait. Should we stand? Sit? Here? There? I was alert to every movement outside the wide front window.

Rick took a phone call and moved to the quieter side of the lobby, by the large fireplace. I fiddled with magazines on a center table, shuffling them and flipping pages without looking. At the sound of Rick laughing, I turned and saw him coming toward me with some people, one of whom was carrying an orchid. Rick was saying my name, and

I realized I was looking at my sister, Carol. She was framed in the firelight, her eyes glistening with tears, and I took in the shape of her face, the tilt of her head, the spray of white blossoms, and threw my arms around her. Carol responded with warmth and acceptance, and I didn't want to let go.

The maître d' interrupted to tell us our group's "other party" had arrived and was in the bar. We peered through the crowd, and I saw my other new sister, Dyanne, coming toward me. I was in awe at the sight of her, and we hugged amid the crush of Saturday night revelers. Strange backs bumped into us, arms reached past us for their drinks. No one noticed the clumsy middle-aged couples whose hugs were not those of old friends but of family finding one another for the very first time.

On the way to our table, we stopped to take photographs. The newly discovered sisters lined up, and husbands snapped away with three iPhones. Our arms around each other, we kept repeating how crazy this was, and Carol and Dyanne told me I was dressed in Shirlie's colors, in her style, and that I stood like her. She was still unreal to me, and I couldn't imagine her, but hearing these similarities excited me.

Dinner was fun. We talked easily and animatedly. I heard Dyanne's husband tell Rick I talked like Shirlie. Everyone told me how much I looked like a younger Shirlie. Carol pointed out that even the stack of bangles I wore was Shirlie's style and later commented that my calm and "demure" personality was like our mother's. Overwhelmed at the parallels they were drawing, I was more curious than ever about my mother.

What was most remarkable about dinner was that even this first experience felt more profound and comfortable than dinner with friends. It felt like family, but how could it? Though I experienced this when I met Larry's family, it still surprised me. Once again, I didn't know these people, yet there was familiarity—the molecular understanding I had spoken of before. I could practically feel cells waking up and recognizing me in these people. Something was happening that would never be undone. A family had welcomed a long-lost member home. This recognition, this knowledge, was permanent and profound, and it happened while we were chatting and passing the butter.

I remember the candlelit dining room and Dyanne's voice, deep and gentle. Her face was softly lit, and a hand-knit scarf lay under her long blonde hair. She was worried about one of her sons that evening and also spoke of her passion for her church. She struck me as genuine, steady, warm, and grounded. There was sadness coming from her, but I felt comfortable and safe with her. She felt like home.

Carol was to my left, animated and beautiful. Svelte and stylish, she wore a dark jacket trimmed with gold buttons, her blonde hair curved gracefully at her shoulders. Her eyes sparkled as she leaned in to tell stories. She was engaged, open, and fun, yet she struck me as a sister in need of a family. I also felt comfortable with her; she felt very familiar.

We sat at a round table in the hushed, deep-green dining room. An arc of candlelight fell over the three sisters, golden and warm—Hollywood couldn't have lit us better. We ate, laughed, stared, and wondered. We didn't know how our lives would change, but we knew they had forever.

The next day I was drained. All I wanted to do was sleep. Friends emailed me wanting to know how it went, but I could barely reply. I was overloaded and needed time to catch up. I struggled to process the past week and kept falling asleep.

By late afternoon, trying to stay awake and function, I sat at my desk, organized a stack of paperwork, and took another look at my email. There was a new one from Dyanne. I assumed she was writing about our dinner last night, and taking a sip of tea as I clicked it open,

I saw Shirlie's name mentioned. Dyanne was writing to tell me Shirlie now wanted to meet me and would leave it to me to initiate the meeting. And just like that, I was swept under again. I couldn't breathe. I couldn't move. God, I didn't have the energy for all of this. It was too much.

She wanted to meet now? She would leave it up to me?

She would have to wait. I needed time. I shut off my computer, whorled into myself, and went back to bed.

A few days later, I emailed Shirlie. "Would you like to have lunch toward the end of the week?"

"I'm busy and fully booked until next week."

"I'll be away then. Maybe we should look to the first week in May?"

"I'll see if I can change something."

The next morning she texted. "I can do lunch tomorrow, the only day I have open. Will that work?"

I stared at the screen, panic rising. *Tomorrow? Just us?* My breath caught in my throat.

"Absolutely."

Not simply "yes" or "sure," but "absolutely"? Why was I being so generous? I embarrassed myself, but never mind that. It was done. I was going to meet my birth mother tomorrow. Alone.

I was terrified. Terrified in a way more profound than anything I'd ever experienced. I felt as if I was jumping off a cliff. My stomach and heart were in free fall, and I was overcome, physically weak, and woozy. Drifting upstairs, I climbed into bed and pulled the covers up as cold sweat spread over me. I trembled and shuddered. Yes, I was anxious, but there was something else I was feeling. Something beyond simple anxiety. What was it?

It was deep, sobbing sorrow that engulfed me and swallowed me whole. A wretched, annihilating grief burned through me, and I wanted to cry like a baby.

This was not a good sign.

What was in the Pandora's box I was about to open?

I couldn't imagine walking into the restaurant the next day. I'd be alone with no one to witness it, replay it with me. No one to take a photograph or share the mind-boggling moment. Yet I knew it would not work otherwise. It needed to be that private, just Shirlie and me. I knew she wouldn't have it any other way.

She wouldn't have it any other way? Why did I agree to that? I was still trying to please her, but part of me was also rising to her challenge. I would go and walk into that restaurant alone.

You don't scare me, bitch.

I'll be there on my own two feet.

See you tomorrow.

My bravado waxed and waned throughout the day. One thing I feared was losing the myth of Shirlie. For most of my life, I imagined her as a kind and welcoming mother, but in recent years I'd been angry with her for rejecting me. Without physical contact, I could hold on to the fantasy that she would be a good mother to me *if only she would meet me.* Or I could stay angry with her for not meeting me. The real woman would be a mix of good and bad, more ordinary and confusing, as actual, live humans always are.

Meanwhile, though I was sixty-one years old, I believed that I, the perpetually good child, could please her and unearth the kind and accepting mother I'd always wanted her to be.

When Rick got home, I told him how scared I was, but he didn't understand. He thought I would be excited and happy to finally meet Shirlie, and since things went so well with Larry, he didn't imagine this being a daunting situation. I needed him to know what I was feeling but had a hard time explaining it. Finally, I read him passages from my journal, and when I finished he reached for my hand with tears in his eyes.

Will came by to see how I was doing; he knew how tense I was. Touched by his empathy, I felt better after our conversation.

Before heading to bed, I took our dog, Hunter, for a walk. It was still and very dark. Remnants of fog floated in the air, and the scent of damp grass rose with each step. As we neared the bottom of the meadow, I talked aloud to Larry, something I hadn't done in years. I told him how much I missed him and wished I could share this Shirlie drama with him. I apologized for not talking to him as often as I once did. I told him I was glad I met him first, and tasted tears as I thanked him for his love and remembered the strength of his hands gripping mine the first and last times I saw him. Looking up into the black sky, I felt cool air across my face, and a sense of peace filled me. I smiled and said, "Thank you, Larry."

CHAPTER TWENTY-THREE

A Long-Overdue Luncheon
2016

The next morning I was surprisingly calm as I prepared for a Garden Club meeting as if that were the day's main event.

When I walked into the kitchen, my housekeeper, Rosa, told me I looked pretty. I thanked her and blurted out, "I'm meeting my biological mother today for the first time!"

She smiled her bright, beautiful smile and gave me a slight nod. "The blood calls."

I was flabbergasted by her words. Yes, that was precisely it. I couldn't believe Rosa understood this instinct, this biological drive to find my long-lost family.

I told her I was nervous. I didn't know what to expect.

"You are about to have an interview with your past," she replied.

I left the house smiling, charmed by Rosa's words.

At the Garden Club meeting, I chatted with friends and participated in club business. Initially impressed with how well I was holding it together, I realized I'd been fooling myself when my stomach lurched midway through the guest speaker's presentation. I was sitting on a folding chair in a church vestry, listening to a gardening lecture when I should have been somewhere freaking out. I checked my watch and realized I'd have to leave before the speaker was through, so when he paused, I stood and apologized for my early departure and heard myself say I was going to meet my birth mother. Clearly my nerves were unraveling, and I was seeking support from every person in the room. There were gasps and wide eyes and smiled best wishes as I turned to go. I took it all with me. I needed every bit.

At the restaurant, I asked the hostess for a nice table by the window, as I was meeting my birth mother for the very first time. Again, I said the words out loud, asking for support from a stranger. Intrigued, the hostess led me to a table by an open window in a bright corner, and I sat, leaving the seat with a better view for Shirlie.

It was quite a few minutes before I saw the hostess approaching me deliberately and ceremoniously, and I realized it was happening. Clutching menus to her chest, she smiled proudly and took each step as if she were about to present royalty. I understood Shirlie was behind her, and although I couldn't see her, I jumped from my seat—this was it! The moment I'd waited for all my life! My birth mother! Everything was a bright flurry, and before I even looked at her, I was hugging her. She was shorter than I imagined, and I was looking down into her curly blonde hair. She stiffened at my embrace, so I let go, my heart falling as we silently stepped away from each other and moved to the table. The hostess looked confused, then turned and walked away, disappointed this wasn't a Hallmark moment.

I looked at Shirlie with tears in my eyes and could see myself in her, though not as much as I'd hoped for; maybe there was a little in the shape of our faces. Shirlie was eighty-one years old, but her skin was unusually smooth, and her blue eyes remarkable. She was wearing the same turquoise I wore to meet my sisters when they told me it was "Shirlie's color."

"You're so beautiful!" The words just tumbled out. I knew she was vain, and didn't intend to pander to her, but was captivated by her face and eyes. Her high school yearbook inscription read, "Angels are painted fair to look like you." She was used to being pretty and responded with a small laugh and polite thanks, the kind of response one might give a stranger. She looked uncomfortable and slightly annoyed as she sat as far back in her chair as possible. Even her head pulled away from me.

Her first words were, "I don't know who you look like. The girls said you look like me, but you don't. In one of the pictures you sent, you looked like Carol, but now you don't look like her at all."

"Well, that photo was ten years and ten pounds ago!" I joked, but she didn't smile, and I was hurt that she didn't see the similarities. A pang ran through me, but I brushed it aside and tried to connect.

We talked for three and a half hours, but it was the kind of conversation you'd have with a colleague. She seemed most comfortable talking about her career in real estate and conservative politics and only briefly veered into anything personal when she told me how her first husband died. I expressed my sympathy for her loss and my admiration of her ability to manage as a widow with five young children. She appreciated that—but something was off. It wasn't appreciation I sensed as much as self-satisfaction or even triumph. She didn't have empathy for me but wanted me to have empathy for her.

There was no more than a passing mention of her childhood and nothing about my siblings or her life raising them. The superficial conversation exhausted me, my chair was uncomfortable, and the back of my legs hurt, but she wasn't showing signs of either wanting to leave or getting honest with me. I couldn't believe this was dragging on. Wasn't she anxious to be done with this meeting?

My phone pinged and Shirlie stiffened. "I left my phone in the car so I wouldn't be disturbed."

"Oh, I have my phone on the table to show you photos of your grandsons and my husband."

She looked surprised that I thought there were any photographs she'd care about. Picking my phone up, I walked to her side of the table and showed her a photo of Rick. No response. Next, I showed her Will and Ben, her grandsons, but she didn't comment on either boy and sat with her hands in her lap. She'd seen the only photos that matter and wasn't interested, so I stopped. As I closed my photo file, she glimpsed one of me at age two and grabbed my phone, peering intently at the picture.

"Did I send you that one?" I asked, not remembering which photos I included in my original letter to her.

"No," she said, turning away from the image. She put the phone down and pushed it away. "No, this doesn't look like any of my children."

My heart hurt. I wish I'd had the guts to say, "Well, Shirlie, I *am* one of your children. I am your firstborn." But I just crumbled a bit more.

Finally, in our last ten minutes, adoption came up. I told her again about wanting to see her face and my desire to learn where I came from. I tried to explain the feeling of being dropped from the sky and needing to meet "my blood." I did so honestly but gently. I didn't want her to feel attacked or blamed, but I wanted her to understand the loss and abandonment adoptees feel, so she might understand why I wanted to meet her. She listened.

"Yes." She smoothed her napkin and looked away. "I have heard the word "abandonment" used when people talk about adoption."

She mentioned adoption as if it were something she'd only read about, not something she'd participated in. "But, if you aren't adopted, you don't think about these kinds of things."

"I realize that, and I'm sure these must seem like strange and almost irrational feelings, but I assure you they are genuine and universal among those who are adopted."

"No, they don't seem irrational. I can understand that."

I was amazed by her responses.

Then she told me I had the mistaken impression there was more of a relationship with Larry than there was, and she was shocked to learn he carried a torch for her all those years. She said this in a way to imply Larry was odd, and I was instantly defensive. I didn't like her dismissing him or trying to diminish me by doing so. The stories Larry told me went beyond casual, and he'd given me photographs and notes of theirs revealing a loving and extended high school relationship.

Shirlie told me she didn't realize she was pregnant until she was six months along when she was whisked off to New Jersey, and "it was all over in ninety days." She said she didn't like to think about it, that it was upsetting and disturbing. I understood but also knew she was lying about her relationship with Larry and her pregnancy timeline.

Finally, the long, strange meeting ended, and we stood to leave. I asked if I could take her picture. "Oh, no, I never take a good picture."

I couldn't leave without a photo of her. Everyone would want to know what she looked like!

"Well, can we take a picture together?"

She reluctantly agreed.

We'd stayed so long that every other table had been cleared and set for dinner—no one was around to take a photo of us. No waiter, hostess, or busboy. The light was grainy, and shadows stretched across the room.

On the way out, I spied a bartender and asked him to take our picture. He snapped a few and hurried back to his post. Shirlie examined the photos, which were awful of both of us. Harsh overhead lighting carved deep shadows in our faces. She looked nothing like the woman who sat before me. I looked more haggard than I felt. She asked me to delete the photos and said she didn't want anyone to see them. She told me we would get together again, and there would be another opportunity for a photo.

I hugged her goodbye, and she patted my back stiffly.

The minute I got home, I received a text from Shirlie asking me to delete the photos, saying no one who saw them would ever forget how awful she looked. They were bad photos, and I didn't like myself in them either, so I agreed to delete them. I wasn't anxious for anyone to see the images but needed concrete proof that we met. I didn't believe there would be another photo opportunity anytime soon, so I kept two. As I swiped across the photos, I saw that she wasn't smiling in any of them. She looked like she was standing in front of a firing squad.

I also realized nothing about us looked remotely like mother and daughter, which is why I really didn't want to show those photos to anyone. It wasn't the shadows on my face; it was that we didn't look enough alike.

Shirlie's text also thanked me for making the meeting easier than she could have imagined and said I was a lovely person, and we would get together again. Her words were stellar, but my radar was buzzing. I didn't believe her.

CHAPTER TWENTY-FOUR

New Brothers

2016

Settling into my car after lunch, I sat perfectly still and silent, as if listening for something. I struggled to make sense of it all, to process the afternoon enough to clear my brain and drive home.

How would I describe this meeting to friends and family?

It wasn't as bad as it could have been. It wasn't antagonistic. She even made a few surprising comments. It was okay, I thought. Pleasant, even.

However, there was absolutely no connection. Nothing like I'd experienced when meeting Larry. But I didn't want to compare them. I tried to accept Shirlie on her terms. Maybe this would build slowly. My God, she was my mother. There had to be a connection between us! I saw this as a start. Yes, we had begun. Optimism drove home with me.

But as I repeated the details to Rick, it became clear that she was still denying me. She'd sat across the table from me for three and a half hours and rebuffed me to my face, repeatedly telling me I didn't look like anyone in her family, which had, clearly, provided her with some sort of relief. She'd been cordial but had made no attempt to connect with me. I was an acceptable lunch companion as long as I wasn't her daughter.

Sorrow flooded in and I began to crash.

Dyanne sent the text that had pinged my phone at lunchtime. She and Carol were anxious to hear how the meeting had gone. I still didn't know what to say, so I shared the basic facts: that it seemed fine on the surface, we'd talked for three and a half hours, but I hadn't felt any connection to her, and it was clear she still needed to deny me.

My sisters were devastated. They hoped Shirlie would open her heart to me, expose the secret, and free a warmer, kinder Shirlie. They'd pinned their own hopes to our lunch. They, too, sought a loving mother. I was losing hope that it would be possible for any of us.

We continued to text all evening. Layering their emotions on mine, my sorrow on theirs, built greater clarity for us all. Our exchange was frank as they shared family stories and asked me questions. They wanted to see a picture of Larry, the man who'd created me with our mother, a man they'd never heard of before. Their first reaction to seeing Larry's photo was that he could have been their father's brother, they looked so much alike. I pulled out the box of photos Larry had given me and found a picture of Larry and Shirlie with their high school friends. Suddenly, I saw something I'd never noticed—an inscription in the lower corner of the photo sleeve, *4-9-53, Larry, Love Forever and Ever, Lee.* (Shirlie had been called Lee in high school.)

That was six months before she became pregnant with me.

I snapped a picture of the inscription and photograph for Carol and Dyanne, proof that there'd been more between Shirlie and Larry than she claimed. They had suspected she was lying about Larry and confirmed that lying was a habit of hers. When we stopped texting, I was so exhausted my brain barely functioned. I tried to bring Rick up to speed on the conversations but could only skim the surface. I was too tired to talk. I couldn't wait to get to bed, and slept fitfully, waking at 5:00 a.m. in acute stress. My body was feeling more than I wanted to admit and demanded I start paying closer attention.

The next day, Rick suggested I get together with my brother, Steven, to meet everyone I'd spoken with. Steven had kindly called me the morning after the siblings received my letter, and I looked forward to meeting him. Though overwhelmed, I felt compelled to pull all the pieces of the family together and invited Steven and his wife, Lauri, to dinner. We'd agreed to meet at a local Italian restaurant because Steven's favorite meal was chicken Parmesan.

On the way to the restaurant, I realized I was going to meet a new family member with absolutely no idea what he looked like. Steven had seen photos of me in the letter I'd sent, and I had one clue about him—he always wore a baseball cap.

Rick and I arrived first and took seats at the table. While Rick studied the menu, I took nervous sips of water, turning every time the door opened. Another rush of cold air, and I turned again. This time, I knew it was Steven. He wore a Yankees cap, but I would have known him anywhere. He looked just like me. I jumped up as they came toward us, and as we embraced, I knew I was hugging my brother. It was that chemistry, that feeling of cells recognizing each other and of coming home. I felt safe.

We chatted about typical family things over dinner, our grown sons (we each have two), jobs, and hobbies, and our conversation was easy and comfortable. We marveled at my appearance in their lives, and Steven's eyes teared up as he empathized with me. He told me he was shocked by Shirlie's behavior and promised to encourage her to get to know me. Steven and Lauri hoped one day we could get the entire extended family together, and it was comforting to have them include me in their vision of the family. I was touched by their desire to make such an effort.

Later, I met my brother Gary; his wife, Barb; and their two sons. I have a lot of nephews—Dyanne, Steven, and Gary each have a family of two boys, just like I do. At a dinner hosted by Steven and Gary, my nephews commented on how much I talked, moved, and looked like Shirlie and made a point of saying how my hands gestured just like hers. I had thought I had Larry's hands, and I didn't know Shirlie well enough to see if they are hers instead. My nephews' enthusiasm was unsettling. It is odd to be closely compared to a woman who doesn't feel like my mother in any way. I wish those comments reinforced a feeling of belonging instead of confusing me about her rejection.

My siblings and their children were open and generous, and I was sorry I hadn't reached out sooner. There was only one brother I'd yet to meet, Bill, who lived in Utah with his wife, Susan, though we'd spoken on the phone, and they were both warm and inclusive.

Sadly, the conversations I had with each of my siblings were loaded with disturbing information. They told me shocking stories about Shirlie's parenting that traumatized each of them. It's not my place to describe that abuse, but it broke my heart. It was clear I was lucky not to have been raised by Shirlie. The more I learned about her, the more horrified I was that I came from her.

After all this drama, I looked forward to going to Nantucket for the Daffodil Festival, an island tradition the last weekend in April. Rick stayed in New Jersey for a golf tournament, but I had plans with girlfriends and hoped going to my happy place would be a distraction and relief. Perhaps being where I felt most anchored would help me process meeting Shirlie and all my new siblings.

Stepping off the plane on Nantucket, the wind whipped hair across my eyes and into my mouth as damp, salty air filled my lungs.

It felt good to be home. I grabbed a cab, and as it turned up our street, I leaned forward to catch the first glimpse of the ocean. It reminded me there was nowhere I'd rather be. When I opened our home's front door, the familiar scents wrapped around me like an old friend's arms, and I felt tremendous relief to be away from the chaos in New Jersey. That night, I climbed into bed, pulled up the crisp sheets, and fell into a deep sleep.

My friend Anne Marie had arranged a group dinner at a popular restaurant in town the following evening. She had a house full of out-of-town guests, and I was happy to enjoy the company of women who knew nothing about the recent events in my life. However, as the evening wore on, my defenses wore down, and jumbled thoughts pressed in that were harder and harder to ignore. By the time dinner was over, I was thoroughly drained and relieved to climb into my car and head home.

The empty, unlit road made me feel more alone and unsettled with each passing mile. Every part of me felt heavy, and it was difficult to lift my arms to turn the steering wheel. Once home, I stumbled out of the car and stood in the driveway for a few minutes to listen to the waves crash on the beach. There were no other sounds in the night air—no voices, no footsteps, just the resonant booming waves. The cold night was still with brilliant stars, and I stood trying to absorb the peace and power of the moment.

With a long exhale, I dragged myself to the door and climbed the stairs to bed. The emotional toll was setting in—my best intentions to escape had failed. I laid my head down and cried through a fitful night, tears tracing along my temples and sticking my cheek to the pillowcase. Come morning, I was spent, and even my view of the ocean didn't help. There was no joy or gratitude. Everything around me was still and silent. I felt like a small child alone in a big house. I struggled to take deep breaths and moved like molasses—it wasn't simply exhaustion. It felt like I was suffocating. I wanted to jump out of my skin, and for the first time ever, I wanted to run away from Nantucket. What was wrong with me?

I needed to go home to New Jersey. I wanted to be with Rick and the boys. Switching my flight to an earlier return, I grabbed my suitcase and headed to the airport. I fought tears all the way home on the plane, as upset to be leaving Nantucket as I was at the thought of staying. Crazy, conflicted feelings ran rampant, chasing around and up and down inside me like trapped animals. I had no idea what to do with them.

Upon landing, I cried for the entire forty-five-minute drive home, and when I arrived, I trudged up to Rick's study and sobbed into his arms. With his simple question, "What's going on?" the words began to flow.

Given my years of searching, I was surprised I didn't want to be related to my birth mother and felt "less than" because I was. She was awful. Denying me to my face was crushing and underscored my sense of unworthiness. I'd imagined warm hugs and the words, "I wanted to keep you but couldn't," or "I always loved you and thought about you." Instead, I felt like a rejected and abandoned child. Curling into the armchair in Rick's study, I sobbed until I was utterly drained.

CHAPTER TWENTY-FIVE

A Family Holiday

2016–2017

A month after meeting Shirlie, it was time to return to Nantucket for the season. I invited Dyanne and Carol to visit me on the island and we scheduled a girls' weekend (no husbands or kids) and looked forward to trying to wrap our heads around this new family. Spending time with Carol and Dyanne gave me a sense of what it would have been like to have blood sisters, each of us different but cut from the same cloth. My sisters and I loved the same colors and shared the same tastes. We understood things about each other, good and bad. We saw things the same way, or, if not, we understood why. It was amazing to feel that connection, the genetic and spiritual knowledge about each other despite having so recently met.

We walked down to The Summer House one evening, an old clapboard inn overlooking the ocean. Our steps crunched on the pebbled front walk lined with pink climbing roses and blue hydrangeas. As we made our way inside, we were met by the summer smells of gin and tonic and sunscreened bodies. We sat on an old wicker sofa, its cushions as flat and musty as you'd expect in any old house by the sea, and watched the crowd swaying arm and arm around the piano as a rollicking rendition of "Sweet Caroline" filled the air. Two women sat on the sofa across from ours and scanned us. One raised her glass, laughed, and shouted over the music, "Well, you can certainly tell that you're all related!"

Dyanne, Carol, and I looked at each other and beamed. The woman had no idea how novel it was for us to hear those words—we looked like three middle-aged sisters who'd spent our lives together.

"Yes! We're sisters!" I shouted. "But we just met each other for the first time a few months ago!"

The woman's eyes widened, she leaned in to hear more, and we took turns telling our story over the clamor of Saturday night at The Summer House.

More than once that summer, I thought of how much Shirlie would appreciate the beauty of 'Sconset and our home and gardens and wished I could share them with her. "If only she could see this beauty. I know we'd bond over it."

Despite all the evidence that Shirlie wanted nothing to do with me, I couldn't let it go. It was as if my very life depended on having a connection with her, which, of course, it did once upon a time. It was like a physical wound I was trying to repair, the abandoned infant in me trying to reconnect with the missing part, my lost mother. I wanted the connection with her to make me whole and affirm who I was. Now that we'd made contact, Shirlie's love and approval seemed within my grasp if I could only figure out how to prove my worthiness.

When I returned to New Jersey in the fall, Carol, Dyanne, and I got together as often as possible. Usually, that meant meeting for lunch on Carol's day off, and we'd linger until the waiters gave us the evil eye. We always parted reluctantly and never tired of saying how astonishing it was to find each other.

As the holidays approached, I wanted to share them with Shirlie's family, to learn their traditions, have them see mine, and create a stronger family bond. With every Christmas decoration placed that year I thought about Shirlie and her family.

The Christmas tree was an art form to me. The shimmer and shadow created a portrait of my family's lives, and I wished I could share it with my new family. Ben's favorite childhood ornament was the Christopher Radko gingerbread man. With its gleaming arms outstretched and red hearts glowing, it hung front and center. Yankee baseball, skiing, and golf ornaments were added as he grew up. Will's favorites were a childhood musical teddy bear, historic Minutemen, Nutcrackers, and the firefighter ornaments we added when he joined a crew. A yellow front-end loader and a carved trout represented Rick's gold mining and fly-fishing hobbies. My special ornaments were gleaming silver hearts Rick and the boys gave me over the years and the stuffed felt ornaments I made the first year Rick and I were married.

The tree filled the room with the crisp snap of pine, hundreds of multicolored lights wove through the boughs so it glowed from within, and there was a delicate silver garland made from thousands of tiny jingle bells, which shivered and sparkled. Handmade Christmas stockings hung by the fire; pine cones, garlands, and white amaryllis decked the halls; and the smell of cinnamon and sugar curled through the house. I wondered about the traditions my new family cherished: What did their trees look like? What were their favorite ornaments? What cookies did they bake? I grew up with Grandma

Leef's Scandinavian Christmas cookie recipes, but what did Shirlie make? Was their family happy at Christmas?

Dyanne and I worked on getting our new family together at least once during the season, but the first mutual date was New Year's Day. Steven, Gary, Dyanne, and their families came to our home, though Shirlie wouldn't join us, and Carol couldn't be there. We served a casual lunch, the kids wandered the property and played pool downstairs, and the adults stood around the kitchen in shifting combinations. I enjoyed conversations with Steven and Gary and their wives, Lauri and Barb, and was grateful for the time with them. I hope they also learned more about me, the latest addition to their family, the surprise from the mother we shared, the mother who had disappointed all of us.

As they said goodbye, Steven thanked us and said, "I'll keep working on Mom, and maybe sometime we can get the whole family together." I was happy to hear Steven refer to us as a family and express again his wish to gather everyone together, though it looked less and less like that would ever happen.

CHAPTER TWENTY-SIX

Remember When

2017

In February, Mom called to say she had something very important to discuss but didn't want to do it in front of my father. She wanted to go somewhere we could talk. This was an unusual request, and I steeled myself for what it might be.

Mom was waiting when I arrived, impatient to get her coat on while hovering close to a manilla folder on the dining room table.

"Hurry and put my coat on me," she directed without even a hello.

Getting Mom into a coat was a tedious process, given her painful shoulders, but once the coat was on, she grabbed the folder and headed for the door. She inched down the two front steps and along the bluestone walk, and when she reached the car, I held her under her arms and placed her into the front seat, buckling her seatbelt while leaving the painful shoulder strap off. Finally behind the wheel, I turned and asked where she wanted to go. She let out a weary sigh and fingered the papers in her lap. "I'm too tired to go to lunch today. Just drive."

With no destination in mind, I drove down their street and turned left onto the Boulevard, the main road through town. We'd gone only a few blocks when she saw one of the large parking lots for the local beach and told me to pull in there. It was a cold winter day. The lot was empty, with ragged winter asphalt all around. I parked at the far edge, closest to the lake. The wind gusted, blowing a chill through the car and setting the water in motion with waves of black and gray. A flash of sun strummed across the surface and drew my eyes to the far side of the lake. I remembered Mom swimming across this lake and how I worried about her going under halfway across, where it was hard to track her bobbing head and stroking arms. People sailed boats around Mountain Lake but didn't usually swim across it. I thought about how physically strong she'd been as I turned in my seat to face her. She held the folder in her gloved hands, which were shaking.

"I hope this doesn't upset you," she said quickly, "but I need to talk to you about your father's and my obituaries and funerals."

That was a shock. While I expected bad news, talking with Mom about their funerals and obituaries caught me off guard. I anticipated taking care of those things one day, but we'd never even broached the subject. My parents never talked about anything personal. While it was a somber subject, her willingness to address it was a welcomed relief. Dad was ninety-six, and Mom was ninety-five. I was glad she was able to tell me their wishes.

"I had my aide take me to Mackey's Funeral Home last week and spoke to the director, who is a good friend. Dad doesn't know I went, and he'd be very upset if he found out. I made all the arrangements and choices. All you'll have to do is pay the bills." She paused for a moment, holding up the manilla folder. "This folder has all the information you need for the church services, what hymns we each like, and what closing Amen we each want."

She placed the folder back on her lap and struggled to pull off her gloves. The file held neatly typed sheets stapled together and scraps of paper with her now shaky printing. Carefully lifting each one, I saw they all required an explanation. Their CVs were also in the folder. Dad's was old and outdated, and it looked incomplete. Mom's was current.

"There is a draft of an obituary for me you can feel free to use." She paused for a minute. "I hope this doesn't frighten you to talk about, but it has to be done." I watched the light on the lake behind her streak all silver and blue.

She laid the last loose paper back in the folder. Looking out over the lake, she said, "What is really important, what you have to get right, is the information for our obituaries. There is a lot, and you have to get all my schools and degrees correct. That is very important." She looked down again at the papers and waited for my acknowledgment.

"Of course, it's not happy to think about, Mom, but I'm glad we could talk about it. I appreciate your giving me all of this."

She seemed satisfied and immediately pulled her gloves back on. "Please take me home now. I'm exhausted. And don't tell your father anything about this conversation. He would be very upset."

"I understand, Mom. Don't worry. I won't say a thing."

I was surprised at how calm I was. This was the first time we'd ever talked about their inevitable deaths. Should I have been more expressive? Not that I ever was—I always stayed calm in the midst of drama. It just seemed to be how I was wired.

We drove back in silence, Mom too exhausted to talk. Once home, we walked, ever so gingerly, up the bluestone path to the redbrick house. The wind was piercing, and I held her tightly until her home health aide took hold to shepherd her inside. Dad was distracted in his study, and I took my leave without going in. Mom didn't want to risk Dad seeing me at all that afternoon.

As I drove away, I thought how odd it was for Mom to ask her home health aide to take her to the funeral home. I was disappointed she hadn't felt comfortable asking me for help, though maybe she didn't want to alarm me, or she didn't want interference from her daughter. She hated it when I took her to appointments and doctors looked past her to me for answers or information. Whatever her reason, the fact I couldn't support her at that time added to my sadness on that strange winter day.

Deciding to run an errand on the way home, I drove the back route out of Mountain Lakes through the neighboring town where Grandma Vincentz had lived. I twisted down the steep hill between the towns, taking the road Mom always worried about when Grandma drove in the dark. Then I crossed the smooth Rockaway River that flooded every spring, past the tall redbrick hospital with its big white cross, and to the other side of the open farm fields toward the small town of Denville.

As I entered town, I impulsively turned down my grandmother's old street, which I hadn't driven in decades. I was curious about the lilac bushes on her property but found no bushes remained at all. A professional building filled her land from corner to corner. I drove around the block to ensure I had the correct address, and yes, there was the post office behind her house, the little park where Santa Land set up every Christmas, and many of her old neighbors' houses. I wondered when her home was torn down, the lilacs lost. Continuing out of town, I crossed the highway and followed roads I hadn't been on since childhood. They snaked up and down hills, through neighborhoods unchanged for decades. Nothing was familiar, but I had a haunting sense of being there as a young girl and pictured Mom driving. Maybe we had a friend or relative who lived there. It felt like a place Mom went with us, not frequently, but occasionally and for some pleasant reason. As I drove, I was aware of pressure building in me. Underneath my calm exterior, something was bubbling up. I was getting farther away from Mom and Dad's house, and increasingly unsettled, and I questioned why I chose this circuitous route, this drive through a past I could barely remember. I should have jumped onto the highway and been done with it. At another of many stop signs in the neighborhood, I slowed the car and glanced down to turn the radio on. Mom's folder was resting on the passenger seat, where she had been sitting minutes before. Her large, wobbly printing covered the folder, and something inside me broke. Tears came in one strong gut punch. I tried to keep driving but couldn't. I was crying so hard I couldn't see the road.

The family that had sheltered and loved me was coming to an end. They were my identity and base. I loved and depended on them. My older brother, Eric, was gone, and now I faced the end of Mom's and Dad's lives. My family was disappearing, the fragile structure was breaking, and that sad and empty feeling snaked through me again.

When I arrived home, I sat down with the folder and pulled the papers out. Dad's information was old and definitely needed to be completed. There was a list of patents and publications from his career as an electrical engineer at ITT, and his favorite hymns were noted, along with the sevenfold Amen he preferred. Mom's information was updated and complete; her CV went on forever. The "draft" she suggested for her obituary included her academic achievements, jobs, and community service. But something was missing, a few somethings. There was no mention of my father or any of her four children. Apparently, we were not an essential part of her legacy.

That reminded me of a call from Mom after she attended the recent funeral of a close friend's husband. Mom was agitated because the entire day had revolved around the husband, Jack, and no one said anything about his wife, Connie. Mom complained that even the grown children were "only talking about their father" and was upset that no one lauded Connie, who Mom viewed as the backbone of the family.

"But Mom," I almost laughed, "it was Jack's funeral! Everyone will say lovely things about Connie when it's her funeral. But this was Jack's day!"

I was confused by her anger until I realized she worried she would not be duly acknowledged at Dad's inevitable funeral. Mom had become vehemently jealous of Dad, of any attention he received from home health aides, friends, and even the family. I chalked it up to age-exaggerated narcissism, but now I know she'd suffered small frontal-lobe strokes, and her ability to see beyond her own needs had greatly diminished. By the time she handed me her "funeral folder," many more unseen strokes had taken their toll. Mom was afraid people wouldn't remember her, and this folder, with her drafted obituary, was her attempt to not be diminished or forgotten. She had spent a lifetime working hard to not be, ever since she was a little girl who felt invisible in front of her severely depressed parents.

CHAPTER TWENTY-SEVEN

Déjà Vu

2017

It was May 2017 when I saw Shirlie again, a year after our first meeting. Dyanne arranged lunch for the three of us, and her presence helped this get-together feel more normal, or as normal as it can when you are sixty-two and meeting your birth mother for the second time in your life.

We settled into a polished mahogany booth, and Dyanne and Shirlie fell into conversation about Dyanne's kids and work. I listened and joined in occasionally, and there were moments that felt so familiar I had to remind myself we hadn't been doing this all our lives. My cells were entirely at ease. Despite Shirlie's reluctance to claim me, my body had found its home. We shared DNA, and this feeling wasn't a choice. It was an innate belonging of blood, molecules, and memory. It was staggering and irrefutable, and I wondered what it would have been like to have had this feeling of connection and affirmation all my life.

I thought of the Facebook photographs of some of my friends' grown adopted children, and how they didn't fit with the family. The differences were glaring. Body types were not the same, coloring was off, and interests didn't jive. The DNA of a different clan had emerged to reveal the inherited talents of another bloodline, the patterns repeated through time along a different family tree, the one they'd been separated from through no choice of their own. I'd look at those Facebook photos and wonder whose families those young adults came from and about how much they didn't know about themselves.

I am who I am, quiet and calm because it's how I was made. Two of my adopted siblings, Eric and Susie, teased me for being too reserved and proper, which made me feel something was wrong with me. Watching myself with Shirlie and Dyanne, I saw our shared demeanor, which Carol and my new nephews commented on the first time we met.

Shirlie and I also had similar tastes and were both collectors. It would have been wonderful to share that. My adopted mother, Audrey, was practical and always chose function over form, making my love of decorating, art, fashion, and gardens seem frivolous. What a surprise to learn it wasn't frivolity. It was my DNA.

As lunch with Shirlie and Dyanne continued, I relaxed into the conversation, sometimes speaking but mostly listening. With Dyanne's prompts, Shirlie talked about her family, her mother (my grandmother), family names, countries of origin, and her older sister. Some of her dates were obviously wrong, and her references to 1954 omitted any mention of her pregnancy or its result, me, sitting right next to her. In her mind, that pregnancy and that baby didn't exist and had no connection to me, the adult woman having lunch with her. As long as she could keep me at arm's length, I was okay. I just couldn't be a member of her family.

Thank goodness for Dyanne. Her presence made lunch as comfortable as possible, so much better than my first meeting with Shirlie. However, while Shirlie was comfortable with Dyanne, she wasn't happy to be with me, and it was mind-boggling to see her navigate those extremes simultaneously. She was relaxed yet guarded and conversed pleasantly with both of us while dismissing me. She could do it without saying a word or behaving rudely—it was masterful nonverbal communication. She played me like a Ping-Pong ball. One moment, I'd think how nice she was, and the next, I'd feel complete rejection. The back-and-forth exhausted me, especially as we sat so close we almost touched. Shirlie was shorter than I and sat slightly forward on the banquette. Her pale blonde hair fell in gentle curls around her face, and stray whisps glowed like a halo in the overhead light. Her cheeks were smooth, her petite nose perfectly shaped, and the turquoise scarf draped around her neck set off her vivid blue eyes. As she moved her hands, bracelets twisted and sparkled on her wrist, so close they were distracting.

The irony of this physical intimacy rattled me. This woman sitting next to me, this virtual stranger, was my mother! I had grown in her body. I was a part of her! A deep shudder rolled through me and goosebumps slid across my skin. It was impossible to process, and I recoiled. I'd spent every day of my life wondering about my mother, searching for her, and now here she was, having iced tea with me in a booth, everything perfectly pleasant as long as I wasn't who I really was. I wished I could hug her, feel warmth from her— feel found.

After lunch, Shirlie said an awkward, stiff goodbye and drove off. Dyanne and I remained in the parking lot for a few minutes. It was one of the first sweltering days of spring. Sun blazed on the asphalt and raised an oily tar smell. I spotted a lilac bush in a nearby yard and focused on its scent instead. Dyanne leaned against her car and said she thought it'd gone well and felt comfortable, despite Shirlie's revisionist history. She believed the entire family could get together one day, just as Steven had hoped. Overall it *had* gone well, but I don't know if Dyanne felt the wall of ice wedged between Shirlie and me. Shirlie put on a good show but was never going to open her heart to me or become a more present and loving mother to my siblings. Still, we all dreamed of Shirlie being something she was not.

Dyanne and I hugged goodbye. I slid my sunglasses on and headed home. But driving along the winding country roads, my spirits fell with each turn. What had just happened? I couldn't make sense of the meeting with Shirlie. Why did I think things were going well one moment, then the next, realized she was still jamming me, keeping me out? I assumed she'd agreed to today's lunch to appease her "real" children, but her message was the same as the first time we'd met: I didn't want you then, I don't want you now, I'm not happy to meet you, you are not mine. She was still denying me to my face. What was wrong with this woman? What was wrong with me?

I couldn't work, read, or even watch TV for three days after that lunch. I didn't want to talk. I didn't want to do anything but sleep. When I was awake, I wandered around the house until the day was done. I often found myself in the living room, where I'd stand in the doorway for a few minutes and stare, not knowing what else to do or why I kept going there. Golden light filled the room, hovering over the soft blues and greens, an embryonic atmosphere that enveloped and calmed me. This is where I'd sat during my first phone call with Shirlie. Is that why I kept returning?

That fall, Dyanne and I made plans to invite Shirlie for lunch at an old inn along the Delaware River in Bucks County, Pennsylvania. It was a two-hour drive in each direction and nerve-wracking to think about being in a car with Shirlie for so long, but I was ever hopeful for another chance with her. I drove, glad for the focus and distraction if things were awkward, but the drive was okay, as Shirlie and Dyanne talked about people and places I didn't know. The countryside was charming, filled with Revolutionary War–era homes and rambling stone walls. The time passed quickly.

The inn had a stunning view of the wide Delaware River, and slow-moving water reflected a cloudless blue sky with a big yellow sun, and bright orange foliage lined the riverbank. Shirlie's mood was polite but tentative, and I couldn't help staring directly at her when she talked with Dyanne across the table or she gazed away at the river. Her profile was pretty, even at eighty-two, with her sweetly shaped nose, pink cheeks, and soft curls. I felt fine if I thought of her as a lovely woman I was out to lunch with. But if I thought of her as my mother, the sharp dissonance between my physical comfort when close to her and the way she iced me out sent a jolt through my body. She rarely looked at me. It was clear I made her uncomfortable. I understood having a baby out of wedlock in 1954 was a traumatic experience, but so was being given away as a baby. We were both a part of this, we'd both been hurt, and I believed we could help each other heal. But she would not welcome me into her life. Despite having known me for over a year, and my positive relationships with her five other children, I was still not wanted. She had looked me in the eye, taken measure of the woman I'd become, and despite my sincerity, dismissed me once again.

CHAPTER TWENTY-EIGHT

Requiem for a Father

2017

That fall, Mom was losing weight and had become legally blind, confused, and angry. Her behavior was increasingly intolerable for Dad and her home health aides. She'd always been critical and demanding, and we assumed age had exacerbated her natural tendencies. Dad, who'd loved her with tremendous patience for over seventy years, met the end of his rope. One day, as Mom berated her aide, Dad walked into the kitchen and said, "I've had about all I can take of this!" He sat at the breakfast table and fingered his empty coffee mug. "No one outside of this family knows what she's really like."

That was the angriest, most critical thing I'd ever heard my father say about Mom. I'd never heard him acknowledge the ugly side of her! But with aides now in their home every day, her behavior was embarrassing and exhausting. There didn't seem to be a gracious bone left in her body. At the time, we had no idea Mom had suffered frontal-lobe strokes.

I didn't ask Dad how he'd tolerated the worst of her throughout their marriage. We didn't share those kinds of conversations, and

I doubt he would have said anything further. She had been wholly devoted to him for seventy years and shared all the activities he loved, from skiing to singing in the choir. Mom managed the kids, organized every vacation, spearheaded their social life, and laughed at every pun he made. She also provided a voice of anger and judgment, which Dad couldn't express alone. She loved my father passionately, and seeing their long love story end with such disappointment broke my heart.

A couple of weeks later, Mom called to tell me Dad had the stomach flu, and she was worried about him. The call surprised me since I'd just been with them, but at ninety-six, changes were neither subtle nor slow. When something shifted, it was seismic. Mom wasn't a reliable source of information anymore, so I jumped in the car to see for myself.

Dad was slumped in their bed, in his undershirt. Dirty covers crumpled around him, and towels were strewn on the floor. The room smelled rank and was unnervingly still. I'd never seen my father look like this in my life—he never stayed in bed. *Ever.* He would never allow himself to be seen by me or anyone else in his undershirt. He was *always* dressed. What was going on here? Just how sick was he?

Mom's diagnosis grossly underplayed what was going on with Dad. He was very ill and had been suffering for a long time, hiding his symptoms from everyone. He was hospitalized and released twice before he became so acutely ill they scheduled exploratory surgery, risky for any ninety-six-year-old.

On the day of Dad's surgery, we brought Mom to the hospital with my sister, Susie; two of her grown children; and my son Ben. We settled in a small waiting room, where Mom sat in a wheelchair, slumped against the metal frame, her bony fingers wrapped around the handles. Unfortunately, Dad's surgery started later and took longer than expected, and Mom became agitated and hungry. Once she focused on dinner, she didn't remember why she was there, so my sister took her home.

As the evening wore on, Ben and I were the only ones remaining. The fluorescent lights hummed overhead, the room was uncomfortably warm, and we stared at the black scuff marks on flesh-colored walls, the molded orange chairs, and the red Coke machine. My body ached, and I thought I'd go mad from waiting. I glanced at Ben. He was so handsome in his suit, the burnished tan of his wingtips resting on the dark blue of his knee. He looked solid and strong, and I was grateful he was there.

At long last, the surgeon came and told us Dad was doing okay with the procedure, but they found cancer everywhere in his abdomen. It blocked his intestines. The surgeon said there was nothing they could do, and Dad had only weeks to live. He pulled out his iPhone and asked me if I wanted to see his photos of the cancer in my father's body. I waved him away. No, I did not. Tears were streaming down my face, and I turned toward Ben, who was wiping tears from his own eyes. The yellow light buzzed around me, and the small room's walls closed in. I couldn't believe I had just received this news. I hugged Ben, and I don't know what I would have done if he hadn't been there. His love and presence held me up at that moment. He'd stuck it out and waited with me—he didn't let me hear this alone. I was so grateful and proud of him.

Rick was in California and arrived home the next day, just as the Thanksgiving weekend began. He asked to be the one to tell Dad about his cancer, to save me from it and Dad from having to watch my face as I broke the news. I told Mom, but I'm not sure how much she absorbed.

As soon as he could be released, the doctor sent Dad home to die. The last few weeks had been a blur of exhaustion and chaos, and now, with Dad at home again, managing his care, and Mom, I was in constant motion. It was the rare moments of rest that allowed fear and loneliness to flood in, often when I got into my car to drive home late at night. One night I called Susie, who lived about an hour from my parents' home, looking to share my anxiety and receive comfort and encouragement. That was unusual for me. I was the caretaker in the family, the listener and the fixer, and had been, especially, for my sister. I spent a great deal of time and effort helping her through life. She was very dependent, bipolar, and a substance abuser. But I was overwhelmed and needed a sibling to listen and care and thought I could count on her. Instead of empathizing, she told me I shouldn't do everything for our parents; it was too much and would kill me. She said her therapist told her we shouldn't be caring for our parents; it was too demanding a job.

What? People care for their dying parents every day! It's what you do! Her incredulous statement enraged me! Who was going to do this, then? Were we supposed to abandon our parents, turn their care over to hired help and let them die alone? If she couldn't help, she should at least support me, not tell me this would kill me! I punched the button to hang up, absolutely speechless. I drove through streaking black rain, reeling from her comments. Tractor trailers blared by, throwing up ghosts of spray, and their powerful headlights bore into my eyes as they careened past. They dodged my car effortlessly and moved ahead with such determination I wondered where they were coming from and how far they had to go. I pressed on in their wake, trying to get home before I fell asleep at the wheel.

My sister sent me an email shortly after that phone call with a note from her therapist. It was, in essence, a "gym excuse" to get her out of helping with Mom and Dad's illness and deaths. He said she shouldn't have anything to do with this process, that she was too fragile. I read the email and reread it to ensure I understood. I was livid. What the hell kind of note was this? What the hell kind of therapist would encourage someone to stay away from their parents' final days? What the hell kind of person *would* stay away from their dying parents? When you are family, you do what you have to do. You rise to the call. You put others before yourself. You Goddamn do unto others as you would have them do unto you. But that was not happening in this family. There was no sibling to share this burden with—Eric was gone, Mark lived far away in Tennessee, and Susie wanted nothing to do with it.

After a week at home, Dad admitted he was in pain and asked me to get him something to help, which meant a call to the hospice nurse for morphine. I sat with Mom to tell her and get her okay. She seemed surprised but listened as I reviewed the plan. "Well, alright, if it will help Dad. We should do that. He asked for it?"

"Yes, Mom. He asked me to get him something for his pain, and he wants it today."

Mom nodded, told me to make the call, and we started the morphine that evening.

The next morning Mom called early, screaming that some woman was at the house to see Dad, and she didn't know who she was. I knew it was the hospice nurse and reassured Mom as I jumped in the car and sped to Mountain Lakes.

Mom sat on the edge of the sofa, turning crumpled Kleenex in her hands, her face hard, eyes flashing. Every fiber of her tiny, emaciated frame coiled in anger and unfurled at me the moment I entered the room. She told me some woman said upsetting things to her (but she couldn't remember what), and we had to get rid of "that woman who was causing trouble and making Dad worse." When I tried to explain what the nurse said, that Dad would likely pass within the week, Mom turned her head away from me like a petulant child, as if my words wouldn't be real if she couldn't see me.

"Just tell me the truth," she demanded.

"I'm trying to, Mom, but you won't listen!" We sat side by side on the sofa. Mom glared straight ahead and told me I'd made all the wrong decisions and they were hurting Dad.

Devastated, I grabbed my phone and ran outside onto the front walk. The day was gray, the air bitter and still, and I kicked at patches of snow stuck on the bluestones, exposing dirt and brown leaves. I called Rick, who was in Salt Lake City for his mother's eighty-sixth birthday. "I can't take it anymore! She is impossible! She's making me crazy!" I was pacing, circling, crunching over mounds of snow, my ankles tipping precariously on buried ice. I could feel the pressure in my head; my face was red hot but my body chilled to the bone. It was hard to breathe. I was scared and felt so very alone. I didn't know how to handle any of this, and the person I should have been facing it with, my mother, was angry and blaming me for what was happening to Dad.

"You should take a break, go home, and get some lunch," Rick suggested. "You can go back in a couple of hours."

It felt strange to leave, even for a little while, but I expected the coming week to be exhausting and needed to steel myself, so I agreed. A break from the tension with Mom was a good idea. We needed to reset. I went inside to tell Mom but found her distracted with no memory of being upset.

Before leaving, I visited with Dad for a few minutes. When I'd arrived earlier, I heard him chatting with the nurse. I was surprised he responded with his usual pleasantries after starting morphine the night before and hoped his pain had lessened. He was sleeping peacefully now, but I stood beside his bed and said, "Hey, Dad, I'm going to run home, but I'll be back shortly. Everything is fine here. I love you. See you in a little bit." I wondered if he was aware of my exchange with Mom in the living room or if he'd heard me screaming on the phone outside. Both were uncharacteristic, and I didn't want to upset him. I stood beside him for a moment more, and as I turned to leave, I thought I heard a slight sound of acknowledgment.

When I returned a few hours later, Mom's aide was cooking dinner while Mom sat waiting at the kitchen table. Chicken was crackling and bubbling, and I smelled baked potatoes. Steam clouded the windows, and the room was uncomfortably warm. I shrugged off my coat and asked, "How's Dad doing?"

The aide looked up from the frying pan, "Good," she said. "He stopped coughing." She pointed her spatula at the baby monitor. That didn't sound right, so I ran to the bedroom. I knew instantly he was gone.

Inching closer and closer to Dad, I prayed there was still a breath and reached out to put my hand on his chest, but it was motionless. Then I touched his forehead. No response. I caught my breath and willed my knees not to buckle. How could this be? Dad had passed in the few hours I'd been gone! This was too fast! We'd only just called hospice yesterday. The nurse said he might pass sometime in the next week! I never expected he would be gone in less than a day and was devastated I hadn't been there with him. My father died alone, with no one by his side. I'd failed him. Why did I leave? I shook my head and took a breath. *Stay calm, stay calm. Handle this. You will have to handle this. There's no one else.* The moment I couldn't imagine facing was here, and I met it alone. *Focus. What should I do?* What had hospice told me to do? There were instructions—*call hospice.*

"I think my father has passed," I said to the unknown person on the other end of the phone. They told me someone would be there in thirty minutes, and as I hung up, I wondered if the nurse might find some sign of life. I needed a few more moments to say goodbye. But for now, Mom needed to know. I would be gentle with her, ease her into this. After all, I wasn't sure.

Mom was still eating dinner, and I pulled out the chair next to her. "Hey, Mom, Dad's not doing well. I've called the nurse to come to check on him." She looked up and said, "Oh, really?" then returned to her dinner.

Now I needed to call Rick. My father had just died, my father was in the house dead, and Rick was not there. He was on the other side of the country. It was surreal, and when Rick answered my call, I could not say it out loud. I whispered the words into the phone: "My father died." Rick sounded so far away, and I felt so alone. I was scared and didn't want to face this. I didn't want to be strong. I wanted somebody else to take over. I wanted to crumble and weep.

When the hospice nurse arrived, Mom shuffled down the hall after her, appearing at the bedroom door just as the nurse removed her stethoscope and shook her head. I put my arms around my mother and told her Dad was gone; she let out a cry and doubled over. Once we settled her back on the sofa, she looked straight ahead and said "I don't want to be here when the funeral home comes. I want to go get ice cream."

Fortunately, Will was not far away, and he rushed to help, bundling Mom off to find an ice cream parlor open on a cold December night.

Later, after the mortician left, I walked through my childhood home, darkening the rooms that would never feel the same again. Turning to pull the front door closed, I noticed the Christmas lights around the big picture window in the living room, the lights Mom and Dad requested so the neighbors across the lake had something nice to look at. They cast an eerie red glow into the night air and broke my heart. I pictured the void of Shadow Lake, black and cold, and remembered how lost and alone I'd felt growing up there. Dad had been the love in this home, and I couldn't imagine it without him.

I wrote Dad's obituary and eulogy without consulting the CV in the folder my mother had given me. I cited his education and career, but there were more important things I wanted the world to remember about Dad—a man who gave the gifts of grace, respect, and appreciation to everyone he encountered.

His eulogy was even more personal, and I read it to my mother when it was finished. I was worried she might be angry or disappointed. I didn't want her to be surprised by it at the funeral. It needed her blessing. I described Dad as a man who intended to elevate others and make them feel better, to allow them dignity, and who was always more concerned with another's welfare than his own. He lightened hearts around him, bestowed moments of peace, and made people laugh. I recalled his description of heaven as how you made others feel while you were still here on earth and quoted Maya Angelou, who wrote, "People will forget what you said, people will forget what you did, but people will never forget how you made them feel." I closed by saying we had been blessed to have been lifted by his deliberate and practiced strength, wisdom, and humor.

When I finished reading, I looked up, and Mom was crying. She said it was beautiful and perfect and then seemed lost in thought. After a few minutes, I asked if she was okay. "Yes," she said softly. "I am just sad you won't be able to say such nice things about me at my funeral."

Dad was cremated, as per his wishes. I am haunted by the image of his body being transported to the crematorium in a flimsy cardboard box and then consumed with flames. It is barbaric, and, maybe most of all, in my mind, it made him vanish. He also requested his ashes be buried in the Memorial Garden at their church, so there is no actual gravesite. His remains are somewhere under the pachysandra. There isn't anywhere I can visit him. I feel like he disappeared entirely. There is no remnant of him left.

Dad's funeral was the first time I'd seen my sister, Susie, since she emailed telling me she couldn't care for our parents. She and her family entered the church sanctuary carrying cups of Starbucks coffee, one of them wearing sweatpants and a hoodie.

As I looked across the church, I was touched to see my biological brother, Sean, and biological sisters, Dyanne and Carol, among the congregation. They came for me, and I needed their support.

There were so many pieces of me in the room that day: my adoptive family, Larry's family, Shirlie's family, and my married family. All the pieces of me together on a day when one of the most important pieces of my life, my father, was gone forever. Rick, Will, and Ben, Sean, Dyanne, and Carol—their love and strength were critical. As for my adoptive family, I felt only distance and disconnection as we scattered around the room.

When the reception ended and the last guests were gone, Rick and I gathered Mom to drive her home. As we pulled up in front of the redbrick house, several vehicles were parked outside, and Mom moaned. "Oh, I don't know if I can take it."

Rick and I each took one of her arms and guided her slowly up the front walk as the December wind whipped through us. It felt so lonely and desolate. Dad was gone, so completely gone after burying his ashes. She was so frail and exhausted. When we reached the front door, we paused to steady her and opened the door to a cloud of marijuana smoke and peals of laughter ringing from the living room. Mom recoiled, confused by who was there and upset by the smoke, which she is highly allergic to. It was my sister and her family making themselves comfortable in Mom's living room, oblivious to the needs of our ninety-five-year-old mother as she returned from burying her husband of seventy years.

CHAPTER TWENTY-NINE

A Distant Relative

2017–2018

A few months after Dad's funeral, Dyanne and I discussed having another lunch with Shirlie. Dyanne was encouraged that our sister, Carol, was in touch with Shirlie again, and both Carol and Shirlie were willing to get together for the first time in seven years. The prospect of being with both of my new sisters and our mother was momentous, and I wanted to make it special. While shopping one day shortly before our lunch, I spotted a silver chain bracelet with a single topaz the color of our familial blue eyes. It would be a perfect gift to memorialize the special reunion planned, and I bought one for each of us. Buying matching gifts for my sisters and mother seemed like one of those "girly" things I'd always wanted to do growing up.

As I drove to lunch, I wondered how Shirlie and Carol would react to being together for the first time after such a long estrangement and what impact my presence would have. We were all nervous as we gathered at the restaurant, everyone a bit stilted, but the tension eased when we settled at the table, and Shirlie, Dyanne, and Carol quickly fell into conversation.

I listened as my mother and sisters shared stories that were part of their lives but not mine, nodding and smiling politely. Jacketed waiters moved in and out, bringing hot popovers, butter, crisp salads, and fresh drinks. The mood was jovial and celebratory, and when my gifts were opened, we put the bracelets on and asked the waiter to take our picture. As lunch progressed, I felt more and more connected to this group of women, this family, primarily because of a kinship with my sisters.

But I still wasn't sparking with Shirlie. She was putting on a good show, though. She fooled me every time with her polite participation. I always thought things were going well, until there was no follow-up, no continued interest. Ultimately, photos of the event revealed the truth, like the firing-squad photos of us taken the day we first met. Shirlie was the only one not smiling in any of them, while I had too bright a smile on my face and eagerly leaned toward her.

I looked at this calm, lovely-looking woman before me and couldn't understand why she remained so cold and distant. Why couldn't she open her heart to me?

My siblings told me my experience of Shirlie didn't differ drastically from theirs. They told me about her failures as a mother, and disturbing stories of what she said and did, including tolerating the abuse her second husband inflicted on them. Her decisions hurt all of us, and I was lucky to escape being raised by her. She would have destroyed me.

At least now, when I closed my eyes, I could see my birth mother's face and understand mine better. I knew why I walked the way I did, why I had certain mannerisms, and where my interests came from. That helped me answer the call of my blood, if not my heart. But I cringed when I noted my physical resemblance to her—the affinity I hoped for all my life now alarmed me. It scared me to share her DNA.

Shirlie was selfish and narrow-minded, cold and cruel. She'd hurt more people than helped, and her habits were foolish and wasteful.

I knew the healthy thing to do, the therapeutic step to take, was to grieve the mother I would never have. Grieve the hug that never came—the kind of hug that sinks deep down into your core. Grieve the look of wonderment over finding me that I never saw. Grieve it all. And move on.

Perhaps she was best seen as a cautionary tale. When I was judgmental, opinionated, or vain, I could think of her and remind myself not to be like her. I couldn't excuse any behavior as random or out-of-character if I knew it was rampant in my birth mother.

Were there any positive traits I could see in Shirlie? Was there another perspective on her life? She was a woman who, in the early 1950s, not only dealt with divorced parents and an alcoholic mother but got pregnant as a teen, gave her baby up for adoption, married within the year, and had a second child nine months later. The marriage was tumultuous, though she went on to have five children. When she was thirty-four years old, she came home from work to find her husband dead from a massive coronary. A young widow with five children to support, she married a man from work who was a raging alcoholic and traumatized everyone in her family. Yet she survived it all. She is a strong woman. I am too. I've powered through some crazy stuff, and I am always surprised when I do. Maybe my ability to keep calm and do what needs to be done comes from her. Perhaps I'd see other strengths or blessings if I knew her better, but it didn't look like I'd have that opportunity. More than my birth mother, Shirlie still felt like a distant relative.

CHAPTER THIRTY

Last Goodbyes

2018

Mom's final Thanksgiving came two weeks before she passed. She was too frail to leave home, so we took Thanksgiving to her. Rick, Will, Ben, and I assembled plates with all the trimmings and took them to Mountain Lakes. Her aide rushed the foil-covered plates to the kitchen and in a few minutes the house smelled like turkey had been slow-roasting all day.

Mom managed only a few bites of food, while Rick and the boys tried to engage her in conversation. She wasn't interested, so they got up to see what projects needed to be done around her house. I remained with her on the sofa, comfortable with the lack of conversation, hoping she felt my presence and support.

She tore at Kleenex, shredding the tissue into clumps. When she raised a mushy handful to her eyes, I realized she was crying.

"What's wrong? What can I do for you?"

She took a ragged breath in. "Nothing. It's just that I want my family."

"Oh, Mom, I know not everyone can be here, but . . ."

She cut me off, and with heartbreaking sobs cried, "Oh, your family is alright, but I want *my* family. I want *my* mother, and *my* father and brothers!" I was shocked at how desperate she sounded. She hadn't mentioned her childhood family in years. They were all long gone.

She was preparing for death. As she lost her tether to this world, she looked back to those with whom she had been physically bonded, those she trusted to care for and protect her when she was young and vulnerable. Watching my mother weep for her childhood family, I thought about the irrefutable, evolutionary bond a child has with their biological kin. The instinctive protection promised by virtue of blood alone. She yearned for the safety and embrace of childhood, like the dying soldier who calls out for his mother on the battlefield.

Those were feelings I missed as an adoptee. That primitive connection. That biological tether. The unconditional support of a clan. I was grateful for the love of my adoptive family, but it wasn't my birthright. As Mom faced death she didn't cry for her adopted children. She wanted those to whom she truly belonged.

———

In December, less than a year after my father, Mom died following a slow and fraught passing. Her searing fear of death surprised me. She was an ordained minister. I assumed she believed in an afterlife and envisioned Dad and Eric waiting for her. But she was terrified of dying, hysterical in the face of it, and many days I'd just sit and hold her. One day I held her for ten hours as she reeled in terror—she believed she was dying that very day. She cried, screamed, and at one point, her endurance failing, she yelled at God, "Take me now!" and pleaded, "Please, please . . ." in a feeble whisper as she contorted her frail body and leaned on me. When her head dropped to my shoulder and her eyes closed, I thought she'd died in my arms, but God didn't take her that day. She'd simply been pushed to her limits.

One night before she passed, I settled next to Mom on the sofa, where she now spent all her time. The large picture window next to us was a sheet of cold black glass, and the poorly lit room was dim and grainy. I felt as if there was grit in my eyes. Mom was tired that evening, and we sat for long stretches without talking. The red velvet wingback chair glowed from the shadows, reminding me of Dad, and a bowl of uneaten oatmeal sat on the tray table, the milky-sweet smell reminding me of childhood breakfasts. I noticed the dish of Hershey's kisses, which she usually gobbled, was still full. At one point, Mom became agitated, squirming in her seat.

"What's wrong, Mom? Can I get you anything?"

"No," she replied, turning her head away from me. "It's just that your being here causes me such anguish."

I was confused. I thought she wanted me there. Maybe she was worried about inconveniencing me, since it was nearly midnight. "It's fine, Mom. I'm not in a hurry. I can stay all night."

"No." She lowered her head and said softly, "Your being here causes me great anguish because you are so patient and calm, just like your father, and it makes me miss him even more. And I also know that once I cross over, I'll never be able to talk to you again, and that breaks my heart."

I put my arms around her and held her as our heads bowed together, and we cried.

"I am telling you goodbye now," she said, "in case I don't get the chance again."

I felt her hair sticking out in all directions, matted from sleeping as much as she did. Her flesh was chilled. Her hands showed more blue veins than skin. Her body was worn out and shutting down. What could I possibly say to comfort her? Pulling her closer, I tried to find words.

I imagined what I'd want to hear from my child at this time and hoped I said something that comforted her, that made her feel loved and appreciated. When we said all we could, we remained in each other's arms until she slowly pulled away and straightened up. She wiped her eyes and fiddled with the Kleenex in her lap.

"I'm okay now," she said. "You should go home and get some sleep. I am fine here. I'll see you tomorrow. Thank you for being here."

I looked at the small, shrunken woman who was my mother, trying to imagine what it was like to face death, leaving everything you knew and loved. "Are you sure, Mom?" I asked, "I can stay all night. It's okay."

"No, no, I'm fine, dear. You go on home. The dog will need you."

I helped her lie down and tucked the blanket around her.

That night was the closest I'd ever been to my mother, and I'm sorry it came so late in her life. But I'm forever grateful we had those moments.

Ten days later, Mom died. I still picture her lying on the sofa, curled on her side like a baby, her cheeks, which had been surprisingly round and rose-colored in recent weeks, already gray and ashen. For the next year, every time I thought of her, that is what I saw, and grief and guilt flooded in. Dying is awful, and she was so frightened. I should have understood more, done more, and been there more. Why hadn't we discussed what mattered—her life, fond memories, Dad? I don't know why she never wanted to talk about those things. Maybe the memories hurt too much. Could I have drawn those stories out? I wish I could return and do more.

I forget that I always did take care of everything for her, yet it was never enough. She was selfish and demanding—to her aides, my father, and me—almost to the bitter end. I know she loved me to the best of her ability, but she wasn't a woman capable of deep emotional connections, nor was she one who enjoyed being a mother. There was an estrangement between us, never true belonging, never a physical bond, and now any hope for ever finding that was gone. And that was the root of my deepest grief.

Mom died in early December 2018, and between her funeral and the holidays, I was in constant motion. My unattended desk was piled high with paperwork, even more so because of documents related to Mom's estate, and as the new year began, I tried to regain my footing and routine, remembering that the world had continued while I grieved for my mother. In a burst of energy, I called my Pilates instructor to arrange a session, eager for movement and camaraderie in the studio.

The next morning, I pulled on my Lululemons and realized I'd lost more weight. The last few months had taken a toll. Chilled to the bone, I layered on a heavy sweater and winter coat. Comforted by the thick padding and warm wool smell, it felt like a good day to start again. I was pleased to reenter the wider world, starting with this Pilates class.

The day was fresh and bright. I narrowed my eyes at the sun and tightened my scarf against the cold. Keys in hand, I slid across the chilly seat of my car. It felt odd that I wasn't rushing to Mom. There was no urgency, and I didn't need to check for a phone charging cord or whether I'd packed enough gluten-free food for an extended stay at her house. I was surprised how unsettling the freedom felt. I headed up the driveway and hesitated at the top. *No, I don't turn right*, I thought. That was the way to Mom. *Today I turn left*, a direction I hadn't traveled for weeks. The neighbors' bright green barn made me smile, as did the perfect blue sky above. The road curved ahead of me, lined with graceful winter branches hanging low like so many hands ushering me in that direction.

The world was peaceful and welcoming, yet as the car moved along, I felt smaller in my seat, like I was shrinking to the size of a child. Every rotation of the slip-smooth steering wheel seemed to take longer, and my coat felt looser. A draft wiggled up. My vision narrowed, and I felt floaty, suddenly detached. A hundred yards down the road, my stomach dropped, and a shiver shot through me, igniting terror. My body acknowledged something I hadn't allowed myself to feel while safely cocooned at home: the day my mother died, I had become an orphan for the second time in my life. My eyes blurred, and my heart pounded as I gripped the wheel, wondering if I would pass out.

The car was moving, fences striated by, and mailboxes dotted in and out, but I couldn't fully function. Would I crash? Should I stop? I eased my foot off the accelerator, my brain scrambling. What was happening to me? What was this feeling? I felt gut-rattlingly alone, as if I were completely on my own in the universe. I was terrified. I wanted to vomit.

I no longer had parents, and I felt like a baby incapable of surviving without them. My brain was reeling. Where was this coming from? Why hadn't I felt this before now? Why hadn't I felt this when my father died? Of course, after Dad died, I still had a parent. I still had Mom and immediately switched to caring for her full-time. Was this what it felt like when you lost your second parent? Everyone loses both parents; it's just part of life. Was I strong enough to handle this? Was this triggering something I'd felt once before when I didn't have words for it? I gasped and took a deep breath—yes, way down deep, there was a terrified baby in me, a baby who remembered what it felt like to be all alone in the world and unsure it would survive. I shook my head as if I could clear the thoughts away. I would not let that overwhelm me. I could manage. I refocused on the steering wheel and felt the car's power in my hands. I was a sixty-four-year-old woman. I was competent. I was loved. I would be okay. I shook my head again, trained my eyes on the road ahead, and drove.

CHAPTER THIRTY-ONE

All of Me

2018–2019

After my parents died, cleaning out the redbrick house fell to me. They'd lived in that house for sixty-five years, and it seemed they'd never thrown anything out. I found rusty, mud-covered Tonka trucks my brother received for Christmas in 1955—home movies show him playing with them under the tree. My father's workbench still held his old cigar boxes full of nuts and bolts, and his bureau held buttons, fingernail clippers, and homemade birthday cards we'd given him as children. My mother's bureau drawers were lined with the quilted-satin organizers I'd glimpsed as a little girl, though her old lady nightgowns and ace bandages now buried the chiffon scarves and silk slips she used to wear.

Coats and hats from the 1960s hung in the front hall closet and reeked of mothballs. I found my father's violin pushed to the back of the top shelf, the leather case splotched with mold. The mahogany breakfront in the dining room held the Lego forts grandchildren had created. Dad nestled them between the champagne coupes for safekeeping, the red and gray plastic at odds with the gold-edged crystal. I'd given Mom a different patterned teacup every year for her birthday because she loved tea, and found them all stacked together, though I'd rarely seen them used. Mom's collection of handmade hostess aprons was in a drawer, among them, my favorite—a blue, ruffled chiffon number with Santa popping out of a rickrack trimmed pocket.

The shelves in Mom's study were crammed with the World Book Encyclopedias I'd used for every school report, along with all her professional books and papers. Boxes of unused greeting cards were everywhere, filed by occasion with Mom's enthusiastic handwritten tabs. In her bottom desk drawer was a spool of the strange, impossibly thin aluminum ribbon that came from my father's lab at ITT, which we used on every gift.

My father's study held teetering piles of books, papers, and scientific journals dating back to the 1940s. I found his diary from 1935 when he was fourteen, his handwriting and sense of humor the same as the man I'd known. Two identical textbooks from the class at Stevens where my parents met sat side by side on the top shelf of his bookcase. One copy was inscribed with Mom's maiden name, the other signed by Dad, and seeing them nestled together in such an honored spot brought tears to my eyes.

The house was dust-covered upstairs and moldy downstairs. My parents' failing eyesight hid the dirt from them in recent years. The basement was the worst, with the smell of oil from the furnace, bleach from the laundry, and mildew mixing. I worked upstairs as much as possible near the large picture window in the living room. It was still winter when I started to clear out the house. Not a leaf obscured the view of the lake or sky, and it was my solace as I sorted and packed my parents' belongings.

I took pictures from the window every day during Mom's last months. There are photos of gray fog hovering so thick you can't see the other side of the lake; fiery sunsets blazing through bare, black trees; and brilliant winter skies, white snow, and blue ice below. The light of the December morning my mother died is my most vivid memory of her passing, and when I see the photograph I took that morning, it stops me cold, and my stomach drops. That was the day my mother died. That was the day this family ended.

Dismantling, deciding, discarding, packing, arranging, signing— emptying a family home is never easy. It was my full-time job for days, weeks, months. Eventually, I called in help: professional cleaners, movers, and a crew of organizers. They had no emotional attachment to anything and helped me keep forward momentum, plowing through it all. The day I called the phone company to dis- connect Mom and Dad's number, I cried—it had been theirs for sixty-five years and was the only phone number I'd ever needed for them, for home.

One spring morning, I arrived before the others, anxious to finish the job. I was still uncomfortable disassembling the house, invading every private space, and tossing away my parent's possessions. I was erasing my family's existence, and once the house was sold, I'd no longer have that touchstone, for better or worse.

I arrived as always, with dread and determination, and dragged myself up the front walk. But that morning, standing among the disheveled moving boxes, something changed. As the early light of spring gathered in the room, a sense of strength rose in me. I actually felt it rise from my legs, up my back, across my shoulders, to the top of my head. The furnishings appeared to shrink, until I felt as if I were standing in a child's playhouse. Unnerved, I stepped outside to take a break. The scent of new grass and damp wood filled the April morning. Dew clung to everything, and sunlight poked through the trees to touch the starting wood ferns. A breeze moved across my skin, and I lifted my face to the sky. Inhaling deeply, I felt the breath spread from my very center, filling every inch of me. I felt solid right down through my feet, their weight pressing into the soft, wet lawn.

A shift had taken place over the months of grieving and packing. I had grown stronger. I'd been freed from the mystery of who
I was and the boundaries of who I was raised to be. As I took apart
my childhood home, there was no more uncertainty. I'd discovered
how I connected to the world and experienced a physical sense of
belonging when I found my blood family. Finding my origins showed
me why I look, think, and act as I do. It also helped me understand
the depth of the primal wound I endured and how necessary it is
to acknowledge the trauma of separation. Without facing the grief
of abandonment and loss of identity, adoptees remain the "adopted
child" forever, deeply affected and living a borrowed life. I had my
full life to live now. It was time to be me, all of me. It hadn't been easy
to integrate the adopted me and the biological me. But as I learned to
accept all that made me, all I was given, and all I survived, I found
love and forgiveness, especially for myself, and felt more authentic
than I ever had.

CHAPTER THIRTY-TWO

Holding My Own
2019–2022

In February 2019, a year after my last lunch with Shirlie, Dyanne, and Carol, Shirlie's husband fell ill. While he was hospitalized, I was respectful, giving Shirlie space and freedom from the stress she felt with me. Her husband died four months later, and though I let her know I was thinking of her, I kept my distance. The weight of grief was fresh in my mind, having lost both Dad and Mom in the past fifteen months.

As the year went on, I sent flowers on holidays, her birthday, and an occasional email or text, to which I received brief, polite replies. I didn't ask to meet, nor did she. Then in March 2020, the COVID-19 pandemic hit, limiting the potential to get together. When the world began to reopen in the summer of 2021, I looked forward to seeing Shirlie again and sent her a special bouquet for her August birthday. However, she asked me to recall the order; she didn't want the flowers. Another consequence of the pandemic: it provided the distance for her to dismiss me from her life once more. She didn't want any reminders of me.

In 2022, on her eighty-seventh birthday, Shirlie was admitted to the hospital with serious health issues, and six weeks after emergency surgery, she was transferred to a nursing home. I was on Nantucket at the time, but Dyanne kept me up to date as she and our siblings managed the complications of our ill, elderly parent. Shirlie became markedly more self-centered, demanding, and cruel, and I wondered if she also had small, unseen strokes as my mother had.

At the beginning of this crisis, Dyanne and I talked about my seeing Shirlie again, as over four years had passed since I had last been with her, including two years of Covid restrictions. Dyanne thought Shirlie might want to make peace with her past, and I fantasized about us having a come-to-Jesus moment, though I worried that seeing me would be unduly stressful for her. But it seemed strange I wouldn't see her as she faced the end of her life.

I traveled to New Jersey in late September, and Dyanne and I arranged to have lunch together. The question of my visiting Shirlie was still open, so we met at an inn near the nursing home. I couldn't wait to wrap my arms around Dyanne. She'd been through hell, and I wanted to tell her how much I loved her.

We sat on the outside patio in the warm September sun, ordered the same salads, and dove into the massive pile of stress Dyanne was shouldering. She looked tired and overwhelmed, and my heart broke for her. I'd had similar experiences caring for my mother and knew how deep they went. Still, it was shocking to hear about Shirlie's frail, deathly appearance at the nursing home and how nasty she was to everyone, especially Dyanne. We found it hard to believe this was happening to her, a woman who always appeared so strong. Her own mother, our Grams, lived to be ninety-six even though she smoked and drank! We expected Shirlie to go on forever, but here she was in a nursing home, unlikely to ever get out.

Dyanne straightened up and leaned back in her chair. "So, do you think you want to see Mom today? I'm worried she'll be mean to you, but I'm happy to take you. It's your choice."

I didn't answer for a minute. The sun was hot, burning my face, a surprise so late in the season, and the aroma of french fries lingered in the air. Autumn bees buzzed our table and circled our heads, and somewhere behind me, children played, their footsteps slapping merrily on the patio, their outdoor laughter like summer itself. For once, I didn't imagine a fairy-tale reunion with Shirlie. I didn't picture her happy to see me or telling me she cared. I envisioned a small, depressing nursing home room that smelled of illness, her lying in bed like a corpse. I imagined her looking at me and yelling for someone to get me out of there, making rude and hurtful comments, or even simply turning her head away until I left. In her current state, any of those things were possible, and I knew I'd be devastated.

Did I want to see Shirlie today? The answer unfurled, rolling through me with sadness but certainty. No, I did not. I wouldn't let her hurt me again. I wouldn't take her abuse. I was done. I accepted that I'd seen my mother for the last time—that we'd already had all we ever would. There was no more.

I smiled at Dyanne and shook my head. "No, no, I don't want to see her. I don't need to put myself through that."

The gold September sun spread across Dyanne's face, igniting her vivid blue eyes. She smiled back at me, nodding sadly. We sat quietly for a few minutes, understanding our hearts were broken by what would never be but also finding relief in letting it go. I was glad to share the moment with her. From her first words to me—"Hello, Janet. This is your sister, Dyanne"—she had given me the love and acceptance our mother never could and helped me find the other half of my heart and myself.

EPILOGUE

Ashes to Ashes: Shirlie's Death
2022

For the next couple of months I held on to my conviction and no longer expected anything from my birth mother. But as her health worsened and the end of her life neared, I wished for one more moment, one final meeting where we might make a genuine connection, such as I'd had with my adopted mother before she passed. But Shirlie was declining too rapidly—there wasn't enough time for her to accept what was happening, and there was no opportunity to say goodbye. A rampant infection took her, and because she also had Covid, she died alone in the hospital.

When Shirlie passed sooner than anyone thought she would, it hurt more than I'd ever imagined it could. Maybe my resolve was not as complete as I thought. I was protecting myself in the present but, in fact, still hoped for a future. And despite forewarning, I was stunned when Dyanne called to tell me the news.

The woman I'd searched for all my life was gone.

I was okay until the day before her funeral when I became unre-
lentingly weepy. I fought back tears at the airport, on my flight, and at
the hotel. I was grieving the mother I barely knew, who did not want
me in her life, but still I was, indeed, grieving my *mother*. The wound
at my center was opening again.

Her ashes were interred graveside on a frigid, sunny November
day in New Jersey, in a plot next to her first husband, who died suddenly at age thirty-four. I found my way to the memorial park and
through the rolling, green fields to the hilltop where two rows of folding chairs sat in front of a freshly dug grave.

As my siblings and other family members arrived, we hugged,
then pulled away and stood nervously, uncertain of what we were
about to experience. One of my sisters-in-law, Barb, gave me an extra-
tight hug and told me how sorry she was for my loss. I was so grateful
for her empathy it was hard to let go of her, though that was only the
second time we'd met.

Barb suggested I help her set up a small table near the grave so
the family could display photos of Shirlie. There were a couple of pictures of Shirlie and my siblings' father and one long faded black-and-
white photo of Shirlie's senior high school class trip to Washington,
DC. It was a large class, and my brother, Gary, pointed to Shirlie in
the crowd. I focused in on her and realized Larry was standing right
next to her. I have another photo from that trip, a small group of
friends in a restaurant, with Shirlie and Larry front and center. The
photo on which Shirlie wrote, "To Larry, All my love forever and
ever, Lee."

I stared at Shirlie and Larry in high school and thought about
how I looked more like Larry and how solidifying it was to see them
together, the two sides of me. It was oddly comforting to have Larry
there with me in this unexpected way.

The young female minister from Dyanne's church arrived to per-
form the service, and as we chatted, I considered telling her that my

mother was also an ordained minister but realized how confusing that might have been. I couldn't seem to speak of that mother, anyway. It felt wrong to bring her up.

Before the service began, I was handed a white gift bag that held a small plastic box with some of Shirlie's ashes. She wanted her ashes scattered in Ireland, and since I was planning to be there within the year for my son Ben's wedding, I could take them. The daughter she didn't want was going to return her to a place she loved. I decided she'd be uncomfortable with that plan and held the bag apologetically.

We took our seats. I sat in the front row of chairs with Dyanne, Steven, and Gary. The tips of my boots rested on the edge of the brass plaque marking the grave of Shirlie's first husband, my siblings' father, and I concentrated on keeping my feet from sliding any further across. On the far side of the plaque there was a small riser draped with an artificial turf blanket, holding a shiny black cardboard box with Shirlie's ashes. Her name and date of death were written across it in bright white lettering.

As the minister read scriptures and spoke of Shirlie, there were muffled sounds of grief around me, and I watched Gary, next to me, wipe tears from his eyes. I tried to hold it together, conscious that everyone else was burying the mother or grandmother who had raised them. They had a history and memories I did not. They lived in the same house and witnessed one another's lives. She served them breakfast before school, fed them dinner every night, argued and laughed with them, and was proud of them. They shared Christmas mornings and family vacations. When Gary and Steven placed their mother's ashes in the ground and told her they loved her and hoped she'd be with their father again, it broke my heart.

We sat and watched as the groundskeeper poured dirt and rocks over the box of ashes, then tapped fresh topsoil into a neat square before he disappeared. We were quiet and still. Tears welled in my eyes, but my sunglasses kept them private.

When we finally stood, I moved to the side, away from the others, and watched siblings approach the fresh dirt and say goodbye to their mother. Nephews and their wives huddled together instinctively, organically. The younger generation. They all had memories to recall, familial humor to lighten the moment. I didn't know any of their family history and, at that moment, didn't feel any part of this family. Yet I physically felt a piece of my center had been removed and buried beneath that fresh earth, lost in the grave with Shirlie.

I stood at the crest of the hill, holding the white paper bag in front of me like an awkward child. Bright fields rolled away to leafless trees, and the cold sun stabbed at my glasses. The wind made me wish for a heavier coat. It was impossible to hold back my grief, and I allowed myself to cry quietly. I didn't feel entitled to express more grief than my siblings, but tears flowed under my sunglasses and dripped down my cheeks. There was a profound ache inside of me.

I realized this was the story of my life. This was what it was to be adopted. I was not, nor ever would be, truly a part of any of these families. Not my mother's. Not my father's. Not my adopted family. I was lucky to have the love and support of Rick and the boys, but I lacked a solid foundation. I worked hard to gather the fragments of my life and piece them together. Harder still to process and integrate all that I learned. And it was that work, and all I had come to know, that strengthened me and held me up as I stood alone on that hill in the cold November sun.

ACKNOWLEDGMENTS

I wanted to write a book about what it *felt* like to be adopted, but not a memoir. My plan was to describe moments that captured the hollow, lonely, frightened feelings I had and present them like poetry, hoping the reader would absorb the emotions and "get it." When wiser minds convinced me that I needed to put such vignettes in context, I cried. I didn't want to "go there"; I didn't want to relive my life. But I wanted to talk about adoption, so, reluctantly, I began this memoir.

Though I didn't expect any surprises, the process of writing brought insights, major shifts, and real transformation. I am grateful for the time and space I had to complete this book but know it wouldn't have happened without the support of some very important people.

Rick, you, more than anyone, believed in and encouraged me. You advocated for a memoir and assured me the stories of my childhood would be of interest when I couldn't imagine why. You listened to endless drafts, and your heartfelt responses confirmed when I was hitting the mark. Along the way you told countless others about my book, and your pride inspired me every time. Your love and support were key ingredients in this book, just as they are in my life.

Thank you to my beloved sons, Will and Ben, for always asking about my progress and applauding my effort. You understood how important this story was to me, and I appreciate your compassion. With Ben's recent marriage to Caroline, I now have a beautiful daughter-in-law who has also been a wonderful supporter and for whom I am so grateful.

My love and thanks to Sean, Gayle, and Jessica, for embracing me when I made a surprise entrance into your lives. You respected the connection I had with Larry and allowed me to see myself as part of a clan, to understand where I came from and who I was. I cherish our time together!

Thank you, also, to Dyanne, Carol, Steven, Gary, and Bill for welcoming me as your sister even when our mother could not. You provided a critical connection to Shirlie and graced me with acceptance. You saved me from the devastation of her denial.

To Dr. Michael Horowitz, thank you for your brilliant guidance to what lay beneath and beyond and for helping me recognize my strength and manage my complicated life!

To Gloria Smith, LCSW, of Children's Aid and Family Services, New Jersey, I am forever indebted to you for finding my birth families and so kindly shepherding me through the mind-boggling experience of search and reunion.

As for my dear friends who were there for me through this journey, your support meant the world to me. Thank you, Janie, for your love and loyalty through everything here and so much more, and thanks also to Nancy, Diane (your video espionage!), Anne Marie, Carolyn, Franci, Jeannie, Kate, Bill, and Peggy.

A special thank you to Rosa, for taking such good care of our home and family, and your profound understanding the day I went to meet my birth mother. Your words, "The blood calls" and "You are about to have an interview with your past," will stay with me forever. I carried your bright smile with me that day.

A big thank-you to Cherie Burns for telling me there was something worth developing in those first eighty pages. You inspired me to keep going!

My most sincere and heartfelt thanks to my writing coach and first editor, Kathryn Kay. Your ability to teach with patience and sensitivity is a gift that took me from eighty pages of prose to this book! You guided me through a million drafts, and I'm grateful for every lesson you shared. You managed to cheer my strengths while pointing out my weaknesses and kept me moving forward when I was discouraged. I had no idea this would take three years, though I think you did!

Dear friends Ed and Barbara Hajim encouraged me to complete this project and generously connected me with publishing whiz Glenn Plaskin. Thank you, Glenn, for your experience and advice, your grand ideas, and introducing me to Forefront Publishing! And thank you to the entire Forefront team, especially Jonathan Merkh, Justin Batt, Jennifer Gingerich, Landon Dickerson, and Hope Innelli.

Finally, thank you to Meryl Moss Media Group for all you have done to get this book out into the world! I hope it starts conversations about the rights of those given away, loss and grief in adoption, the biology of belonging and identity, and why love is not always enough to extinguish the pain.